AF522542

Captain Mani's War

Captain Mani's War

PRS Mani

Edited by Dr. Inderjeet Mani

JUGGERNAUT BOOKS
C-I-128, First Floor, Sangam Vihar, Near Holi Chowk,
New Delhi 110080, India

First published by Juggernaut Books 2026

10 9 8 7 6 5 4 3 2 1

P-ISBN: 9789353452629
E-ISBN: 9789353456214

Typeset in Adobe Caslon Pro

Printed at Thomson Press India Private Limited

To my parents, Saraswathi Mani and PRS Mani,
who taught us kindness and perseverance.

Contents

Introduction

In March 1944, the Japanese invaded northeast India. There followed some of the fiercest battles of the Second World War (1939–1945), with as many as 60,000 Japanese and more than 17,000 Allied soldiers killed. The battles of Imphal and Kohima marked Japan's greatest land defeat of the War, shattering its ambitions to invade India and turning the tide in the Burma campaign. While the Allied 14th Army was staffed with British soldiers as well as many trained soldiers from the traditional Indian fighting clans, it was the first time recruits from all over India were tested. They more than proved their mettle. As my father, PRS Mani (1915–2011), wrote: "For the first time since several hundreds of years, Indian troops have fought united on their own soil resisting a ruthless foreign invader. The heroism, valour, and courage of the Indian troops, true to their tradition, rose to an epic form here and men from all parts of India and its neighbours—

from distant Nepal to the remotest corner of the Madras province—took their share in this great effort."

At the time of the Japanese invasion, my father worked for All India Radio (AIR). That year, he left his broadcasting job to become a public relations officer with the rank of Captain in the 14th Army, reporting on the Battle of Manipur, the Allied advance through Burma and the surrender in Singapore.

He subsequently travelled with the Southeast Asian Command in Java, where he built friendships with the leaders of the Indonesian freedom movement and helped them. Throughout his war reporting, covering 1944–1946, he lived closely with infantrymen, artillery units, cavalry regiments, patrols, raiding columns, and many service corps units. His extremely vivid dispatches, distributed by the army's public relations department and relayed in Indian and British media (including the BBC) are the only eyewitness accounts of these battles written by an embedded Indian war correspondent.

Born in 1915 in Chittoor, Madras Presidency, PRS Mani grew up in a Tamil household steeped in nationalist fervour. After completing his BA from Madras Christian College in 1937, PRS was drawn to Jawaharlal Nehru's vision of democratic socialism. By 1939, he had joined AIR in Madras as an announcer, where his work caught the attention of AIR's leadership in Delhi. He moved to Delhi in 1942 to work on wartime programmes beamed to Indian residents in Southeast Asia before joining the army and beginning his dispatches.

What makes Captain Mani's account uniquely important is not only its historical significance as the sole perspective from an embedded Indian journalist but also its extraordinary literary quality. His prose is stylish and evocative, bringing the chaos, courage, and complexity of war vividly to life on the page. Through close observation and cinematic detail, he captures not just the sweep of battles but also the texture of daily life – the sounds, smells, fears, and camaraderie of men at war. This combination of journalistic immediacy and literary craft imbues his dispatches with a power rarely found in military reporting.

As a reporter for the British Indian Army, my father's journalistic dispatches reflect an underlying tension between his Indian nationalist sympathy for those shaking off the colonial yoke and his journalistic duty to serve British interests. This duality captures the profound complexity faced by Indian soldiers themselves – fighting valiantly against a formidable Japanese enemy while simultaneously aware of the growing nationalist movement at home demanding independence from the very British Empire they served at the front.

The Indian troops were caught in an impossible position: defending their homeland from invasion while wearing the uniform of their colonizers. Captain Mani's writing gives voice to these contradictions with remarkable honesty and nuance. All his war dispatches, while he was a military officer, were censored by the British. In protest against British actions in Indonesia, he resigned his commission there and became a correspondent for the *Free Press Journal* and an Indonesian news agency. He later joined India's foreign service at Nehru's invitation, serving in diplomatic posts across the world until his retirement in 1973.

After his death, his journalistic work drew the interest of historian Professor Heather Goodall, who wrote articles about his war writings,[1] and also hosted some of them at the University of Technology, Sydney.[2] India's National Archives organized an exhibition in May 2013 in Delhi, and his accounts were featured in Goodall's book *Beyond Borders*. Other historians, including Srinath Raghavan in *India's War*, have also made extensive use of his materials.

PRS Mani's writings are highly relevant to the current trend among historians seeking to undo the complete erasure of South Asians' contributions to the great wars of the twentieth century. His work is unique in the way it portrays not only distinguished officers but also ordinary soldiers and recruits, including mule drivers, medics, cooks, and mechanics. He also emphasizes the origins of various fighters and their regiments, from remote corners of the North-West Frontier Province to Chittagong in erstwhile East Bengal and the deep south of India. Equally striking is the teamwork among soldiers of different religions, including the extraordinary valour of Muslim soldiers. In the context of India's recent battles with Pakistan, this account of a united, multicultural, pre-Partition India coming together in the fight for freedom also seems extremely significant.

This book is primarily based on PRS Mani's typewritten dispatches from Northeast India, Burma, Malaya, Singapore, and Java. Many of these were produced under British censorship and a measure of self-censorship while working for the British Indian Army.[3] I have also relied on his uncensored work from that period, including handwritten personal diaries[4] and reminiscences, *Free Press Journal* articles from Indonesia, Burma, and Malaya,[5] and extracts from his book The *Story of the Indonesian Revolution*[6] and his autobiography *Look Up and Aim High*.[7]

As in Martha Gellhorn's reportage, PRS uses interiority and close observation to evoke lived experiences. His uncensored writings reveal ethical conflicts, tactical errors, atrocities, defections, censorship, casteism, and other contentious aspects of the wartime experience. Together, his writings recover a suppressed Indian perspective on the War while offering a broader commentary on censorship, propaganda, and divided loyalties.

To make his voice shine through for modern readers, I have edited my father's writing in various ways: converting many dispatches to a more informal officialese-free narrative register; improving spelling, punctuation, and phraseology; replacing politically incorrect terms; and standardizing names and abbreviations.* To enhance overall coherence, I have summarized many of the dispatches and other writings,** and introduced narrative bridges that include scenic renderings, biographical information, and recapitulations of the military and historical background of unfolding events, based on established accounts and archival material from the Liddell

---

*PRS would often take notes during campaigns, and when in a safe place, would consolidate them into a series of dispatches. There was thus sometimes a delay between the events and PRS's filing a report. The chapter titles and section headings reflect the chronology in terms of the times of the battle event occurrences.

**Some of the verbatim dispatches have been italicized to convey a sense of live reportage however, for ease of reading, most others are in plain text.

Hart Centre for Military Archives at King's College London.[8] The book thus includes editorial reconstruction as well as verbatim quotation.

To make the book even more accessible to readers unfamiliar with the history of this period, I begin with my historical overview. For those interested in the life of PRS Mani, I have appended a brief biography at the end.

I am grateful to historians who provided helpful advice when I started this project: retired Indian Air Force Officer Ranna Chinna, Professor Santanu Das of Oxford, and Professor Diya Gupta of the University of London. My family and I owe a debt to Professor Heather Goodall; this book would not be possible without her tireless efforts to draw attention to and preserve my father's wartime writings. I am thankful to my paternal aunt Mrs. Girija Karthikeyan for more on my father's background; my brother Dr. Ranjit Mani for his counsel; my son Kailash Mani for valuable feedback; and Chiki Sarkar and her team at Juggernaut Books for many helpful suggestions.

1944 battlefield picture of PRS Mani

Historical Overview

While many Indians are taught about foreign invaders, few are aware of the Japanese invasion and the valiant battles that were fought during the Second World War to save India from occupation.

In the spring of 1944, as nearly 80,000 Japanese troops crossed into India's Northeast, my father, PRS Mani, landed in the area carrying a notebook and a revolver. The battles he witnessed would become among the fiercest of the war. To fully understand what he saw, we must look back two years to the chain of events that led the Japanese to push their forces across India's sacred frontier.

The Japanese Sweep Across Southeast Asia

On December 7, 1941, the Japanese launched a surprise attack on the US Pacific Fleet at Pearl Harbor in Hawaii. The attack included nearly 350 aircraft, comprising more than 100 dive bombers, even more level bombers (many armed with aerial torpedoes), and around 75 Zero fighters. Within a day, as the US declared war on Japan, Lieutenant General Tomoyuki Yamashita's 25th Army – comprising the 5th and 18th divisions and the Imperial Guards Division – began the assault on Malaya, crossing into Kota Baru and sweeping through southern Thailand at Singora and Pattani.

In Malaya, the 11th Indian Infantry Division and elements of the 8th Australian Division resisted fiercely. At Jitra, the 11th endured relentless Japanese assaults before being outflanked and forced to withdraw. At Kampar Ridge, the 8th Indian Infantry Brigade, the 5/14th Punjab Regiment, and the 2/1st Gurkha Rifles inflicted heavy casualties on the enemy but could not halt the advance. By February 1942, Japanese forces had crossed the Perak and Selangor rivers and were bearing down on Singapore.

Indian units, including the 1/5th Mahratta Light Infantry and 1/12th Frontier Force Regiment, defended the Johor–Singapore Causeway and northern Johor. At Bukit Timah, the 1/17th Dogras and 1st Malaya Infantry Brigade mounted a counter-attack that slowed the Japanese 18th Division, but enemy artillery proved overwhelming. On February 15, 1942, Singapore fell.

Lieutenant General Yamashita accepted the surrender of over 80,000 Allied troops, including tens of thousands of Indians who became prisoners of war (POWs) or joined the Indian National Army (INA).

Japan's next target was Burma. In January 1942, Lieutenant General Shōjirō Iida's 15th Army, led by the 55th and 33rd Divisions, and later reinforced by the 18th and 56th, advanced towards Rangoon. Lieutenant General William Slim's Burma Corps – the 1st Burma and 17th Indian Divisions, supported by General Sun Li-jen's Chinese Yunnan forces – fought desperate delaying actions. At Yenangyaung, the Chinese 38th Division rescued the 1st Armoured Brigade and parts of the First Burma Division at terrible cost as the Allies retreated towards the Chindwin River. The British abandoned Rangoon on March 7–8, 1942, demolishing the port and oil installations to deny them to the enemy. The Japanese 15th Army occupied the city immediately and severed the Burma Road, the vital Allied supply line stretching from Lashio, Burma, to Kunming, China. Allied remnants fell back towards the Chindwin River and Assam.

In mere months, Japan had conquered Hong Kong, the Philippines, New Guinea, the Dutch East Indies (Indonesia), Malaya, French Indo-China (Cambodia, Laos, and Vietnam), and Burma, while already controlling

Manchuria, Formosa (Taiwan), and Korea, and bringing Siam (Thailand) under its influence. This conquest came with brutal occupation, with prison camps marked by famine, forced labour, and execution, while endless streams of refugees fled across vast territories.

Alarmed that India would be the next domino to fall, the British stepped up recruitment. From 200,000 troops in 1939, the British Indian Army swelled to nearly 2.5 million. It would be this expanded force, with personnel recruited from all corners of India, that would face the Japanese invasion in March 1944.

The Counteroffensive Begins

From 1942 to 1943, the Allies prepared their counter-attack. In Burma's Arakan, the 7th Indian Division clashed with the Japanese 55th Division in savage fighting at the Ngakyedauk Pass and Mayu Range, involving hand-to-hand combat, with ambushes, booby traps and machine-gun nests blocking every advance.

In northern Burma, Indian and Chinese forces, including the Chinese 38th Division, moved into attack positions. Units like the 1/7 Gurkha Rifles fought ferocious engagements amid the thick jungle canopy and monsoon weather, which limited air support. Burmese Kachin and

Karen guerrillas harassed Japanese convoys and provided vital intelligence.

As 1943 drew to a close, the Japanese prepared their own offensive. Lieutenant General Renya Mutaguchi, commanding the 15th Army, began planning Operation U-Go with the INA's contingents under Netaji Subhas Chandra Bose and his officers, including Colonels Shah Nawaz Khan and Shaukat Hayat Malik. The 31st Division, under Lieutenant General Kōtoku Satō, and the 33rd Division, under Lieutenant General Genzō Yanagida, trained in jungle infiltration tactics. Engineers and supply units massed at Homalin, Kalemyo, and Tiddim in Burma, stockpiling material and charting jungle tracks.

The stage was set for Japan's great gamble: the invasion of India.

Operation U-Go: The Invasion of India

In March 1944, the unthinkable happened. The Japanese 15th Army swept across the Chindwin River in Burma and pressed into India. Their mission: seize Imphal and Kohima, cut the Dimapur–Imphal road and strike at the heart of Allied defences. With them came units of the INA, including Khan's Subhas Brigade and Malik's Bahadur Group.

For Indians, the war was no longer distant thunder. Thousands of barely trained recruits – farmers, labourers, clerks, and students – were rushed along with seasoned soldiers to the eastern hills to face an enemy hardened by years of conquest. The fate of India hung in the balance.

The Japanese attacked along three axes. Satō's 31st Division pushed towards Kohima. Lieutenant General Masafumi Yamauchi's 15th Division pressed in the direction of Tamu and Palel. Yanagida's 33rd Division raced along the Tiddim–Imphal road, their columns moving to capture airstrips and strategic crossroads before the Allies could regroup.

By March 14, the Japanese 33rd Division had penetrated behind the 17th Indian Division, forcing the 48th Indian Brigade to withdraw tactically. From March 21 to March 26, the surrounded 50th Indian Parachute Brigade withstood six days of intense assault at Sangshak against overwhelming Japanese forces, suffering roughly 585 casualties.

By early April, Japanese forces had besieged Kohima while pressing into the Shenam–Palel sector near Imphal. Villages like Kanglatongbi – where PRS Mani's narrative begins – were fiercely defended by lightly armed Indian troops who repelled assaults and safeguarded vital ammunition. From April 8 to April 22, intense fighting at the Shenam Saddle, including Scraggy Hill and Crete East and West, saw Indian battalions withstand relentless Japanese night attacks and hand-to-hand combat.

On April 13, the Japanese captured Nungshigum Ridge, threatening Imphal's airfield. The 5th Indian Division, supported by the 3rd Carabiniers, counter-attacked and regained it. The following day, the INA's Bahadur Group reached Moirang and briefly hoisted its Azad Hind flag, only to be driven out by the 17th and 23rd Indian Divisions.

At Kohima, the siege reached its critical point. The garrison – including the Assam Regiment, 4th Battalion Royal West Kent Regiment, and attached units – was squeezed into a tiny defensive zone around the deputy commissioner's bungalow and the tennis court. Japanese positions were a few yards away, and both sides of the court saw vicious hand-to-hand combat until relief arrived on April 18.

By early May, the Japanese advance was collapsing. Hunger, disease, and fractured supply lines had crippled their troops. On May 20–21, the enemy launched a final assault at Red Hill near Bishenpur. Still, the 5th Indian Division, with the help of the 32nd Indian Brigade and 254th Tank Brigade, managed to crush the attack.

On June 22, columns from Kohima and Imphal met at Milestone 109, 7 miles from Kanglatongbi, reopening the Dimapur–Imphal road. Mutaguchi officially called off Operation U-Go on July 3, 1944.

The battles of Imphal and Kohima marked Japan's most significant land defeat of the war. British and Indian losses approached 18,000, while Japanese and INA casualties neared 65,000. The campaign destroyed any Japanese hopes of conquering India forever. General Slim later called it "the greatest defeat the Japanese Army had ever suffered."

For the Indian troops who fought there – Punjabis, Gurkhas, Tamils, Pathans, and others – it was not merely the Empire's war but their own. Few then imagined that this invasion would become a crucible of Indian unity, with recruits from all corners of the subcontinent fighting together for the first time in centuries. It changed forever the lives of those who survived, and my father, both a witness and a participant, was no exception.

The Pursuit Through Burma

The victory in India had been won at terrible cost, yet the campaign was far from over. The exhausted Indian troops had much more fighting to do, but this time they had the upper hand.

After mid-1944, the Japanese retreat across Burma became a desperate exodus under relentless pressure. Through choking dust and monsoon downpours, columns of Indian infantry advanced without respite, and PRS travelled with them.

The 17th and 5th Indian Divisions, backed by the 254th and 255th Tank Brigades, Royal Indian Engineers and Gurkha reconnaissance teams, pursued the enemy without pause. Each Japanese defensive stand only slowed the inevitable as Indian forces pressed through devastated roads, demolished bridges and dense jungle. PRS's account uniquely documents this chase across Burma.

In the Arakan and Tenasserim regions, the 7th Indian Division liberated coastal settlements and cleared river routes. The 15th Indian Corps, including the 25th Indian Division, reopened critical supply lines. Engineers rebuilt bridges destroyed by retreating Japanese units, ensuring Allied tanks, artillery and infantry could advance without pause. Gurkha and Rajput battalions stormed fortified heights and river crossings with unflinching resolve, frequently engaging in brutal hand-to-hand combat.

By early 1945, surviving elements of the Japanese 28th and 33rd armies were retreating through Burma towards Thailand. Indian formations hunted them along the Tenasserim coastline and southern Burma, seizing key locations, eliminating scattered resistance and denying the enemy any opportunity to consolidate. The 1/7 Gurkha Rifles, 1/5 Mahratta Light Infantry, 2/7 Rajputs and 3/6 Gurkha Rifles, aided by Allied air and naval strikes, struck with precision and ferocity.

The last major engagement, the Battle of the Sittang Bend, took place from July to August 1945. On August 6, the United States detonated an atomic bomb over Hiroshima; Nagasaki received another on August 9. On August 15, 1945, Emperor Hirohito broadcast Japan's unconditional surrender to the nation. The official surrender and recapture of Singapore occurred on September 12, 1945.

An Asian power had been defeated. But the map of Asia was about to be redrawn again as new countries sought independence from colonial overlords. My father's journey as an embedded journalist took him next with the Allied South East Asian Command to Java, where freedom itself was under siege.

Indonesia: From Occupation to Revolution

For over 300 years, the Indonesian archipelago was ruled as the Dutch East Indies. This long period of Dutch control ended abruptly when Japan invaded in 1942, forcing the Dutch to surrender on March 9. The country endured three years of Japanese occupation. After Japan's defeat in August 1945, Indonesia faced a power vacuum, and local leaders quickly declared independence.

Soon after, British and Indian troops arrived under Allied orders to disarm Japanese forces and free prisoners, acting as a bridge between the Japanese surrender and Dutch attempts to return. The British also brought along Dutch colonial officials seeking to reassert control. This sparked a struggle between the newly formed Indonesian Republic and the Dutch, who were initially supported by the British military, leading to the Indonesian National Revolution.

The Battle of Surabaya

The Battle of Surabaya was the largest and most pivotal clash of that revolution. Minor skirmishes in October 1945 escalated into a full-scale confrontation on November 10, 1945. Around 20,000 trained troops from the Indonesian People's Security Army, supported by tens of thousands of militia members and young volunteers, defended the city against better-equipped British and Indian forces.

Tensions had boiled over after British planes dropped leaflets on October 27 ordering Indonesians to surrender their weapons, contradicting earlier agreements with the local British commander, Brigadier A.W.S. Mallaby. Fighting quickly erupted, and Mallaby's death near the Red Bridge on October 30 prompted British retaliation with a large-scale offensive.

Led by Major General Robert Mansergh, the British demanded unconditional surrender. The defenders refused. On November 10, British forces launched a massive assault involving naval bombardments, air strikes and 6,000 troops with tanks and artillery. Brutal urban combat raged for three weeks, as thousands more Allied troops joined the fight. Despite being heavily outmatched, Indonesian fighters resisted fiercely, suffering an estimated 6,000 to 16,000 casualties before the city fell. British and Indian forces had around 1,000 casualties.

Despite being a military defeat for the Indonesian Republicans, the battle became a powerful symbol of national resistance. Surabaya fell, but it only fanned the flames of revolutionary zeal. The Indonesian defence galvanized national and international support for independence, convincing the British they could not effectively support the Dutch. The British withdrew by November 1946; the Dutch finally transferred sovereignty to Indonesia in December 1949.

For PRS Mani, witnessing this struggle marked a turning point in his life, from an embedded war correspondent supporting a colonial power to a champion of Indonesia's freedom movement. Disgusted by British atrocities and sympathetic to nationalist stirrings, he resigned his commission. His journey from Imphal to Surabaya marked chapters in the same story: the twilight of Empire and the dawn of independence across Asia.

1

The War from Delhi[1]

February 1942–March 1944

Since the beginning of the war, the British had watched with disbelief as one Southeast Asian colony after another toppled to the Japanese. The collapse of British Burma in particular triggered a panicked exodus. Over half a million civilians fled through jungle paths and mountain passes. Disease, hunger, and ambushes by hostile groups claimed nearly 100,000 of them.

Determined to prevent India from following the same path, the British expanded the Indian Army dramatically, from under 200,000 soldiers in 1939 to nearly 2 million by the time I joined the Army in 1944. It was the largest "volunteer army" ever. The traditional recruiting grounds had been exhausted. Men were now being drawn in from the deep south, from fishing villages and farm plots. The poor, the landless, the illiterate were recruited, with posters at post offices and bus stands advertising the advantages of becoming a soldier:

> *ALL INDIAN SOLDIERS SHOULD KNOW THIS:*
>
> *An Indian soldier on Field Service Overseas who has been in the army for 12 months or more earns a total of Rs. 38. Overseas, in hard cash, the Sepoy receives Rs. 33-38, the Lance Naik (Lance Corporal) Rs. 35-38, the Naik (Corporal) Rs. 46-48, and the Havildar (Sergeant) Rs. 49-53. In addition to this he is fed, clothed and accommodated free, receives free medical attention and electricity, free travel when granted furlough, and travel concessions when granted leave, At a conservative estimate these concessions represent in kind at least Rs. 21 per month to the man not on Field Service and a correspondingly larger amount to the man on Field or Overseas Service.*

These sums, modest as they may seem now, were enough to justify enlistment for many who had never handled a rifle. Most would not become soldiers in the classic sense. They would carry loads, manage provisions, cook meals, manage animals. Yet even these men, untrained in combat, were at times called to the line with little more than faith and borrowed courage. They showed exemplary courage, which I think reflects both the character of our people and the discipline of the Army.

The reader may want to know what it was like for the families of those men. What were the scenes at train stations? Did the wives and children cry? Did mothers try to hold back their departing sons? Of course they did. Most of the men were leaving home for the first time, travelling into a dangerous and uncertain future. But there was also eagerness, a sense of duty, not only to country, but to family. Food was scarce. So was work. The army offered both. And behind the stoicism, I believe, was a quiet pride.

My path to war had been different. In 1939, I joined AIR in Madras, while still studying law. My earliest assignment was to monitor how Indian listeners were responding to broadcasts from Nazi Germany and Soviet Russia. We were in a war of ideas long before the shells began falling. Some Indians, particularly those sympathetic to Bose or the Hindu Mahasabha, found themselves drawn to the Axis message. AIR countered with its own campaigns, trying to win minds as much as hearts.

In 1942, I was transferred to the AIR headquarters in Delhi, to work under Lionel Fieldon, an upper-class

Englishman who was something of a wit and dandy, and Professor Syed "Patras" Bokhari, later a distinguished Pakistani diplomat. Fieldon was regarded as "colorful," which was a code word for homosexual; indeed, at the time, he was in a relationship with Patras's brother.[2] But in our journalistic and political circles, homosexuality was more a matter of gossip and there was no sense of persecution. As for me, my main job was to broadcast in English and Tamil to overseas Indians living in Southeast Asia, many of whom had been influenced by Bose. I also reported on the many other events that were transforming our country.

That August, I was in Delhi when Gandhi and Nehru were arrested for launching the Quit India movement. I had the good fortune of meeting both men before, and I would have followed them anywhere my job required. In those weeks, more than 60,000 Indians were rounded up. Soldiers were ordered to fire on civilians. And we, the journalists, were instructed to say nothing. Official silence sat like a stone on everything we saw. Yet the underground Congress Radio managed to bypass the censors, getting the story out while our own microphones remained mute.

At AIR in Delhi, I wrote dispatches, read reports, and listened to German and Japanese broadcasts addressed to

Indians, trying not to wince at their outright falsehoods. I was having a pretty good time at it. In late 1943, Sir Frederick James summoned me for a meeting. He was a member of the Legislature and I had often announced his discourses on AIR. James suggested, with characteristic British understatement, that I should go to see "how the war was shaping up and report on it."[3] I was to be recruited into the Public Relations Department of the Army with an emergency commission.

On March 8, 1944, I was still in Delhi, waiting for the Army bureaucracy to complete the necessary formalities, when everything changed suddenly. That day, the Japanese invaded India. Key formations of the 80,000-strong Japanese 15th Army entered the Manipur area, accompanied by the Indian National Army.

Some INA men had been Japanese prisoners of war, while others had volunteered. Subhas Chandra Bose believed Japan could help India achieve independence. The strategy was pragmatic, and Bose, who styled himself Netaji after Mussolini's *Il Duce*, was sympathetic to fascism as well as socialism. I found that for some Indian soldiers, there was little difference between imperial and fascist masters. And yet they chose to fight, giving it their best.

Operation U-Go was Japan's name for their campaign. The 15th Army commander General Renya Mutaguchi's aim was to seize Imphal and push further into British India, hoping to incite revolt. His subordinates expressed concern, but he remained committed. On the Allied side, General William Slim, commanding the British 14th Army, had been waiting for the attack, while consolidating forces around Imphal. He had learned his lesson well after his defeat in Burma.

The bureaucracy suddenly woke up. I was swiftly given my Captain's commission. Provided with a revolver, some rudimentary military training and a day's harrowing ordeal with a parachute, I was sent to the front with the 14th Army to start my reporting.

My instructions were clear. As a journalist attached to the Public Relations Directorate, I was told my role was to uplift the morale of the troops, of the families back home, and to increase support for the war effort. We were required to follow the maxims of Dusty Miller, whose words echoed in my ears like a mad tinnitus:

"You will never get a chap to fight, if he's got something on his mind"; so said 'Dusty' Miller, famous boxer and Army trainer. True for the Ring; far truer for the Big Ring we're in to-day. To-day, YOU officers, British and Indian, are true trainers and YOURS is the task of taking those "somethings" off the mind of each soldier by understanding, by interest, by sympathy and by explanation.[4]

The Army PR Directorate had made it clear that war correspondents should emphasize enemy losses and of course our gains, highlighting the achievements of our officers. This was even more important because of the relentless propaganda from the other side, sometimes delivered via special leaflet bombs that fluttered from the sky like confetti.

Like any fighting force, the Japanese were also subject to their own propaganda. General Mutagachi addressed his crack 33rd Division as follows:[5]

"The coming battle will decide the success or failure of the war in Asia. Regarding death as something lighter than a feather, you soldiers must seize Imphal. You must expect that the division will be annihilated. Rewards and punishments must be given on the spot. A soldier who puts up a good show must be decorated, a man guilty of misconduct must be punished. In order to keep bright the honor of his Unit, a Commander may have to use his sword as a weapon of execution, shameful though it may be to shed the blood of one's own soldiers on the battlefield and though the shirker may be worth no more than a horse's backside."

I was a writer and broadcaster, someone used to fighting the information war on the air waves, and now I was being dropped into a real war. The prospect was terrifying, but it was my job, and duty.[6]

To You The English Soldiers!

You are like fishes caught in a net, without an outlet. The only faith left for you is Death alone. When we think and give consideration about your loving wives, parents and brothers we could never carry on inhuman-like actions. Therefore stop your useless resistance. Throw down your arms, and surrender. It is then that we will guarantee your lives and will treat you according to the International Law.

How to Surrender to the Jpanese Forces

1. The surrenderers are required to come hoisting some white cloth or holding up both hands.
2. Carry the rifle on the shoulder upside down.
3. Show this bill to the Japanese soldier.

Nippon Army.

此ノ證携行者ハ投降者ニツキ保護ヲ加ヘラレタシ

大日本軍

Japanese "air-mail" propaganda leaflet[7]

2

The Manipur Front[1]

April–June 1944

The battle at Kanglatongbi in 1944 was critical in defending the Imphal–Kohima road. After the Japanese 15th Division's 60th Regiment captured a British supply dump, ordnance personnel fought a fierce action on the night of April 6–7, repulsing Japanese attackers with Bren gun fire. The 63rd Brigade held the sector until the Fifth Indian Division took over in early May, gradually clearing Japanese positions through repeated small-scale actions. Forces from Kohima and Imphal finally linked up at Milestone 109 on June 22, ending the siege. The stand at Kanglatongbi bought crucial time for reinforcements and helped turn the tide of the campaign.

The war in Manipur was not only one of swift advances or bold maneuvers, but also a test of holding one's ground, of enduring violence and suffering over seemingly endless days and nights. I had arrived as an observer, a hastily commissioned and unprepared Captain, and I soon found myself in the thick of battle.

War changes its actors forever. Instead of the conscientious yet carefree broadcaster I had been, I became something entirely different that I couldn't recognize. I was not quite a warrior but a man of war, and a brother to the steadfast band who labored without complaint, whether it was fighting, hauling, and manning equipment, clearing roads, managing animals, preparing food, or tending to the wounded and dying.

Among this new family, I began to see that heroism was no more or less than the slow, persistent courage of ordinary men doing their duty in impossible conditions. The victories along the way were measured not only in territory regained but in our refusal to yield. As one ridge or command post gave way and another loomed, there were stories still to come, of silent night ambushes, mules threading impossible roads, officers and medics braving floods and fire alike, and men who turned every small act of duty into a testament of courage. The battles ahead would be won by the quiet bravery of ordinary, hardworking people whose feats remain largely unsung.

Kanglatongbi under Fire

Kanglatongbi was a small and otherwise obscure village on the Imphal–Kohima road north of Imphal. It became a key battleground when General Mutaguchi's 15th Army, specifically the 15th Division under Yamauchi, attacked it in their advance southwards. By early April 1944, General Mutaguchi's pincers had been closing. The 31st Division reached Kohima on April 4, beginning a siege. Their 15th and 33rd Divisions pressed into the Shenam–Palel sector around Imphal.

At Kanglatongbi, on April 6–7, Allied personnel from the 221 Advance Ordnance Depot, lightly armed but supported by infantry and engineers, repelled repeated enemy assaults with rifles, grenades, and improvised defenses. They evacuated or destroyed vital ammunition, keeping the road open.

The troops I encountered were already battle-weary, as they had been fighting all over for weeks. The 17th Indian Division, called the Black Cats due to their badges, had just finished retreating from March 13 to April 4 from their forward position at Tiddim in Burma. It was a grueling journey of over 120 miles through mountainous terrain north to the Imphal Plain, all the while facing almost continuous attacks from the Japanese 33rd Division. Their trials went unsung, but brought to my mind Xenophon's *Anabasis*.*

Thirty-five miles to the north, the Battle of Sangshak had raged for a whole week in late March. The 50th Indian Parachute Brigade, including the 152nd Indian and 153rd Gurkha Parachute Battalions, and supported by the 4/5th Mahratta Light Infantry, held an isolated hill against the Japanese 31st Division. Outnumbered and surrounded, they managed to resist for six days, losing as many as 585 men.

Yet even after these harrowing physical and emotional experiences, our soldiers behaved normally. Their movements were businesslike, adjusting wheels, scraping mud off the rifles, lifting stretchers, and, when not too late, diving into bunkers. Around them the fighting was now everywhere, in ditches, under tarps, beside mule trains, among ration tins, and behind mess tents. The uniforms were stained and torn and many of the freshers looked lost, for they were on their first campaign and

---

*Personal reminiscence. Xenophon's *Anabasis* is the narrative of the retreat of more than 10,000 Greek mercenaries at the end of the fifth century BCE.

without adequate training for the terrain. Some of the men were not conventional soldiers but porters, drivers, clerks, and mule handlers. And some were using their rifles for the first time in action.

Improvisation was common, based on the Indian approach of *jugaad*. A sepoy rewired a truck's ignition using a metal spoon. Punctures were fixed with slices of worn rubber boots. Shiny ration tins were used to signal landing sites for airdrops. Spent shell casings were used to carry salt, and leftover grease from the kitchen was used to power lamps.

Most of the time people somehow carried on based on courage and common sense. A mule handler guided his animals under fire with quiet murmurs and a stick. I saw a Pathan carry his wounded brother without calling for help. Another soldier dragged a box of mortar shells up a near-vertical incline. There was weariness, and a sense that work needed to get done, and done very carefully and with wisdom. As our Tamil *Tirukkural* teaches us, *true valor lies in restraint born of fearlessness*; without it, fearlessness becomes recklessness. I learned a great deal about valor from watching the ordinary labors of our fellow men, as well as their feats of daring.

One evening, I met Sepoy James Elliah, a Madrasi from Visakhapatnam. Dust-caked, his rifle slung low, he offered me a cheroot. He told me about the night several weeks earlier when his unit, where he was serving as a bearer, received orders to evacuate the Kanglatongbi depot. They moved 150 tons of rations, mortar shells, and ammunition by hand under darkness and in complete silence. Once finished, they blasted the bunkers. The Japanese arrived shortly after.

That night, Elliah slept in a trench, pistol wrapped in a filthy sandbag. He snored, keeping me awake, but it was a peaceful sound that rose and fell with an occasional shudder, as if some of the trauma of the day was finally being relieved by the balm of sleep. The war was filled with such small moments, intimate, absurd, often terrifying. But the larger currents moved relentlessly on.[2]

General Slim's Strategy

Before the Japanese arrived, an obvious Allied option was to cross the Chindwin and attack the enemy first. Another choice was to hold the Japanese off in the Tiddim region in the Chin Hills to the southwest of Imphal and fight them when they tried to traverse the Chindwin. But in both cases the British would be hampered by the poor lines of communication behind them and the fact that they would be vastly outnumbered.

Slim embodied yet another principle that our ancestors taught us in the Kural: *Let decisions come only after deep, repeated thinking*. He instead chose to concentrate the 4th Corps in the Imphal plain and fight the enemy on ground of our own choosing. To the Japanese, it looked like yet another Allied retreat, but it was a trap.

Accordingly, the 17th Indian Division or Black Cats, led by Major-General D. T. "Punch" Cowan, guarded the approach from Tiddim in the southwest, though they had to retreat. Major-General Douglas Gracey's 20th Indian Division oversaw the Kabaw Valley to the east. The 23rd Indian Division under Major-General Ouvry Roberts was based at Ukhrul to the northeast, where the relentless momentum of the Japanese advance was compared by a senior British officer to a colony of ants on the move.

The battles I witnessed were attritional. Hills and ridges changed hands repeatedly. There was firing but also hand-to-hand fighting, at which both Gurkhas and Japanese excelled. The Gurkhas used their kukris for quick chops at the neck or slashing off a raised enemy arm. The Japanese stuck to their bayonets, aiming for direct piercing of the heart or liver. Injuries were often fatal.

The units fought with little rest. The 5th and 7th Indian Divisions held key positions. The Black Cats retreated under pressure from Tiddim, covering 120 miles, mostly on foot. They returned lean and fatigued, but still cohesive. General Slim re-equipped them and sent them back into the field. I often saw him on the frontline, occupied with logistics details and plans.

General Slim was not from the upper classes, and unlike the British officers serving under him, had not been to any of the famous British boarding schools. Being a former commander of a close-knit Gurkha battalion, his concern for his men led to admiration, and some indeed called him *Uncle Bill.*

Our ranks were linguistically diverse. Orders were translated in real-time, and miscommunication was common. Patrols advanced through thickets. Signalmen repaired communications under fire. Artillery units operated in terrain hostile to heavy equipment. Roads ended mid-slope. Men pulled the heavy guns forward by rope. Mules, many of them American-bred, carried the rest. I heard a handler trying out foreign-sounding commands on the mules, just for a joke.[3] We all knew that what mattered most was tone: harsh orders with occasional kindnesses were understood well by both serving animals and men.

Though the Japanese Zeroes enjoyed strafing us, the skies were mostly under British RAF control. Air-dropped supplies from our C-47s rarely landed where intended.

Parachutes caught in trees or drifted into ravines, though many were quickly recovered.

The ground was a different story. The jungle threats were quiet, for mines lay carefully concealed beneath leaves, waiting patiently for a single careless step. Knowing that enemy snipers could easily blend into the foliage, we advanced carefully with a peculiar prowling gait. Our bayonets and grenades saw more use than rifles, and for hand-to-hand combat, the soldiers used whatever was at hand. The Gurkhas of course had their kukris, and some of the Sikhs carried kirpans; others made do with bayonets and knives. Razor blades were favored by some of the Scottish streetfighter regiments, who kept the blades ensconced in a potato in their pockets.[4]

The Brits called the INA soldiers Jiffs, meaning Japanese-Indian 5th Column. They were sent in early by the Japanese, and deserted from time to time, in increasing numbers once the fight grew worse.

Their behavior was in marked contrast to the Japanese, who at this stage were extremely disciplined and efficient. At times, the Japanese even called out to us in Urdu, hoping to confuse our lines, but their accents always gave them away. They did manage to capture our men, and the outcome was usually bad. After seizing one of their camps, our soldiers found a mess cook with his eyes gouged out.

Other prisoners had been bayoneted.[5] I will not dwell on Japanese atrocities here as they have been described at length elsewhere, but suffice it to say, their cruelty knew no limits, driven by blind obedience to their Emperor. Still, we held to our own code of conduct with our prisoners, most of the time.

General Slim made it a point to visit the men in their trenches. He asked sappers what tools they needed. He stood beside us, noting who was exhausted and who had gone without sleep, and ordered rest and rotations. He was a good man and was friendly during my interviews. It was a sad fact that a few British men who really cared about us sometimes didn't seem enough. Yet we fought together as one team.

The Indians on our side were not fighting to save the Empire. Many were volunteers, and had joined to support their families. Once inside, they fought for each other, for their fellow men in the trenches and the *nullah*s.

I fought with them, for a nation not yet born in freedom. I knew that it was destiny and even karma that had brought us to the battlefield. To stand our ground, to hold the line for what might still become, felt like the highest calling. And my own duty was to report on the truth.

Kanglatongbi Heroes

A journalist never sleeps without filing his report. Who were the men I should write about? I started, naturally, with the British.

When their supply of hand grenades ran short, a resourceful Eton schoolboy with a Reinforcement Camp made fresh ones from old cigarette tins to hurl at the Japanese at Kanglatongbi, Major E.I. Hamilton Parkes, a Royal Engineer, used nearly 50 "Players" tins with a large quantity of broken glass and gelignite to make his grenades which had a deadly effect on the Japanese.

Then there was Lieutenant David Sparkes, Calcutta 13th Frontier Force Rifles, of 93, Gypsy Lane, Headington, Oxford.

He had been a commando in the Luftwaffen naval engagement, and he now led a party of Mahrattas into the perimeter of the NW sector which the Japanese attacked, and they killed nearly 20 of the enemy, with our tanks also helping out. Finally he threw the enemy out, along the way capturing a Japanese LMG (Light Machine Gun) and two swords covered with blood.

A few Japanese foraging for food near the Engineers Officers' Mess were killed. Of two more Japanese who were lurking near the British Other Rank mess (the messes were of course segregated by rank and color), one gave himself up and the other was killed later.

General Mutaguchi had planned to feed his troops with cattle driven from Burma across the Chindwin river, but most of the animals had starved to death from lack of forage. As a result, they had only a quarter of the rations needed to last the four months of fighting that went on in Manipur. It was a tragedy on both sides, but of course I couldn't show any sympathy for Japanese stomachs and the slaughter of enemy soldiers foraging for food.

What about Major Norman Sinclair, 7th Baluch? He had been educated in Holland where he was working formerly in a steel firm, and his wife now lived in Karachi.

Major Sinclair was seeing action for the first time in command of the SE sector of the box and inflicted large casualties on the enemy. He maintained the fire discipline at a high level after an initial bad start since most of the troops were seeing action for the first time. In addition to organizing and sending out patrols, Major Sinclair was the last man to leave the position when they later withdrew. He stayed behind to make sure that everything was scorched.

What I was writing was used for propaganda, but every word of it was true.

I could also not forget Captain Leslie Clements, who wanted to see action and got more than he bargained for.

Like a trout reaching out for its first May-fly, Captain Leslie Clements, Indian Electrical and Mechanical Engineers, of 63 Brunswick Place, Hove, Brighton, was recently rocketed out of a tank through the driver's hatch, and none the worse for it and with a smile over his strange experience. *Attached as Light Aid Detachment (L.A.D.) to a cavalry unit, he had gone out to watch a battle near Kanglatongbi. He was asking for a job and quite suddenly he was led to rescue a tank banked up in a nullah (dry gulch) by the driver who had lost his direction. When Captain Clements was driving back the tank to the rear, about 30 yards from the nullah he heard a terrific rear explosion and the next moment he saw himself flung out of the tank. The tank had run over a mine—the only mine in the area.*

I had dwelled enough on the doings of the British, who were certainly deserving of praise. As soldiers, they showed true courage and cleverness. But now it was time for me to do justice to Indians. I began with the valiant evacuation of the ammo depot and the rescue of huge quantities of vital ammunition:

After keeping vigil every night for nearly a week and working throughout the day, Reinforcement Camp No. 20 at MS IIO received orders at 2200 hours on March 31 to move and take up new defense positions at Kanglatongbi nearly 7 miles away. It was a pitch dark night and no lights could be used owing to the near proximity of the Japanese. Working the whole night and the following day, British and Indian Sikhs, Mahrattas and Madrasis assisted in evacuating nearly 150 tons of stores, reserve rations for 14 days for the 2300 men and large quantities of ammunition including 3000 x 3" mortar bombs and a quarter million rounds leaving nothing to the enemy. All bunkers and defensive positions were completely destroyed.

Captain G. Sethuram had been born not far from my hometown of Chittoor in the Madras Presidency. He found himself and 150 reinforcements surrounded by darkness with the Japanese circling around them. Then a flurry of red tracers shot towards them in the night sky. One of his men called out in fear, and Sethuram, who was standing nearby, put his rifle on the man's cheek and told him in Tamil to *vaay moodu,* in other words, to shut his gob.

On April 4, Captain G. Sethuram, 3rd Madras Regiment, of Odayur village, Chidambaram taluk, South Arcot district, a graduate of the Presidency College, Madras, was defending an IGH (Indian General Hospital) area with 150 Madrasis. They were all reinforcements to the 3rd Madras Regiment on their way to join their battalion. In the night after he had ordered his men to stand to, at about 0130 hours red tracers came in their direction from about 300 yards in the north, completely illuminating the dark sky. They kept quiet and for the next three hours more flares appeared from every other direction in turn.

"This led me to believe that the enemy was all round us but since we had kept quiet they didn't spot us. The patrols I sent out at dawn could not find the enemy and they must have disappeared into the jungles."

The next night he and his men were defending the southern sector of the Garrison Engineer's area at Kanglatongbi when at about 0200 hours the Japanese began their attack. Using a nullah in front of his position as a covered approach, the enemy, nearly a platoon strong, attacked from behind in small parties. The silence of the night was disturbed by their 2" mortar fire and machine gun fire and their shouts which lasted the whole time.

"We did not open fire as we could not see them. Since we were in bunkers and trenches their fire did not cause us any harm and as we kept quiet the Japanese who came within 100 yards of us moved away to attack another position."

Again the next day when the enemy attacked his position early in the morning in pouring rain, Captain Sethuram and his men had been standing to for the whole night. A party of 30 or 40 Japanese approached from the nullah firing at random and on all sides, to ascertain dispositions. When the enemy came to within 100 yards of them, Captain Sethuram and his men who had been quiet all the while were about to open up when they found that the Japanese had once again disappeared.

A battle without communication lines usually spells death. One night, under relentless shellfire, the line between two forward command posts in Kanglatongbi went dead. Signalman Lance Naik V. Anthony listened to the crackle of the handset, then set it down. There was no contact with the forward box, no confirmation of orders, no way to call for help if the Japanese attacked. Anthony didn't wait for orders. He grabbed his coil bag and motioned to three other Signalmen: Faquir Mohammad, Sanwar Shah, and Shah Hussain. They went into the night without lights, sometimes crawling with their hands outstretched to hunt for the broken thread of wire among the roots and puddles.

Devotion to duty in the face of heavy enemy fire was the example set by a Madrasi Lance Naik of the Indian Signals and three of his men. Lance Naik V. Anthony, No. 12294 Signalman Faquir Mohd., No.61568 Signalman Sanwar Shah and No. 56898 Shah Hussain were serving with a unit which was attacked by the Japanese at Kanglatongbi early in April. A telephone wire between one sub-sector HQ and the fortified command post Box HQ was out by fire from enemy guns and mortars. In the pitch dark Anthony and his men kept moving under shell fire from the enemy and feeling their way over the snapped wire, joined the cut pieces together again and re-established communication. They proceeded with their work undeterred even though shells were bursting all around and very close to them. They have been recommended for awards.

I ended with a tribute to my friend Sepoy James Elliah (who I believe did not survive the war):

A complete nonchalant indifference to enemy fire was shown by a Madrasi sepoy who went into deep slumber although Japanese shells were bursting all around him, writes an Indian Army Observer. Sepoy Boddy James Elliah of Mallipula St, Visakhapatnam, was one of the bearers serving in a reinforcement camp which was attacked by the enemy at Kanglatongbi. Not prepared to lose his sleep whatever the Japanese might do, tying a piece of cloth round his head in typical Madrasi fashion and keeping his officer's loaded pistol close to him, Sepoy Elliah stretched himself and slept quietly for the whole night even though enemy shells and mortars were bursting only 20 yards from him.

Sepoy Elliah left his school to join the army and is a cheerful lad with a smile always on his face.

How to Embrace War

In war, truth is precious, but should it, as Winston Churchill opined, "always be attended by a bodyguard of lies"? On the Imphal front, I soon became aware of the efforts of our own propaganda units in broadcasting to the Japanese and the INA. The Indian Field Broadcasting Units (IFBUs) operated from the battle front in the Imphal theatre and suffered severe casualties, along with the Mahratta troops sent to guard them. The Japanese troops listened to IFBU broadcasts, and captured Japanese documents showed that the broadcasts did lower their morale. (The main impact was on the INA, achieving in one case the surrender of an entire INA brigade.)

Sometimes the effect on our troops by our own commanders' reports were of concern. I heard the case of my fellow war-correspondent, the South African-born Major George Steer, Commander of the IFBU.[6] He had reported in the daily Platoon Sheet that two hill positions, Ralph Hill and one near Nippon Peak, had been occupied by the enemy. Brigadier Stuart Greeves, commander of the 80th Indian Infantry Brigade, summoned Steer, who said he received the information from another officer and confirmed it from yet another officer. Greeves said no such positions had been taken, and Steer was reprimanded and forced to apologize to all concerned. From what I heard, it was far from clear that Steer was mistaken. Battlefield "truth" was quickly contested, even by our own command.

There were also numerous instances of officers being relieved of their command for tactical military mistakes, for losing their heads and retreating when they shouldn't have, or taking the wrong route in the middle of a jungle. Another officer, as I recall, was depressed and unsure how long he could hold a position on the feature called Crete. Greeves spent a great deal of time trying to convince him that things were better than they seemed and that persistence was the only solution. And yet Brigadier Greeves himself was unsure what would really work.[7] Battles are often won based on luck and gut instincts.

I have always considered war as a necessary evil. I had once believed, too, in the idea of a just war. That latter belief wore thin. In Manipur, *jus ad bellum* began to feel like a noble fiction, language concealing the bloodiness the earth had already witnessed. Whether civilian or soldier, violence violates the first duty of conscience: to act with heart. As the Mahatma said:

Nonviolence is not a garment to be put on and off at will. Its seat is in the heart, and it must be an inseparable part of our being.

How does one reconcile the ties to one's nation and its civilization with a love for living beings, the latter no matter which side the humans involved belong to? This is the dilemma explored so brilliantly in the *Bhagavad Gita* more than 2,000 years ago. It was the same struggle that led the Emperor Ashoka to renounce war after his victory at the Battle of Kalinga in the Third Century BC. Of course, Ashoka still retained his Empire and proclaimed its glory.

Morale and Entertainment on the Front (April–May 1944)

Within a few months of arriving, my uniform was filthy and I had already lost some of my hair due to stress and constantly wearing a sweaty cap or helmet.

One of their Own

Though I held the nominal rank of Captain, our men treated me as one of their own. On quiet evenings, once their glasses were filled with rum, they laughed and made silly jokes, in Hindustani, Punjabi, Bengali, and Tamil. The more tense things got, the more they seemed to jest, which was probably a kind of psychological defense.

It was these high-spirited men who carried the day, for they, not the propaganda pamphlets, were the true builders of morale. I came across fierce Punjabi jawans from the famed Rajendra Sikhs, of the 1st Patiala Regiment, dressed as dancing girls singing rural Punjabi songs of love and dancing to the rhythm of an improvised tabla. In times of war, men starved for female company will often take on these roles.[8] Now and then the real dancing girls of Manipur would visit the troops and entertain us with folk dances.

I also saw Madrasi sepoys enacting pieces from our Ramayana epic in Tamil in an open-air theatre. They seemed to be carrying make-up articles with them wherever they went, so fond were they of the stage. We also had board games like Ludo and Parcheesi and playing cards to while away time when things were quiet and our duties were done. The mundane always coexists with the extreme, as Auden showed in his marvelous poem[9] written in 1938 on the eve of World War Two, called *Musée des Beaux Arts*:

...

In Brueghel's Icarus, for instance: how everything turns away
Quite leisurely from the disaster; the ploughman may
Have heard the splash, the forsaken cry,
But for him it was not an important failure; the sun shone
As it had to on the white legs disappearing into the green

Water; and the expensive delicate ship that must have seen
Something amazing, a boy falling out of the sky,
Had somewhere to get to and sailed calmly on.

Liquor too played its part in war. I had not been a drinking man earlier, not even in college. That changed at the front. Rum dulled the edge, letting men (and the occasional woman nurse or auxiliary) speak freely, laugh briefly, and feel, for a few hours, less alone. Its importance was such that the Corps Commander approved the creation of an Officer's Club in Imphal. It opened with a dance, attended by hundreds of male officers and an unrecorded number of women. The Club also included a lounge, card room, billiards room, dining room, and of course, a well-stocked bar. But celebration had its limits. Several incidents of drunken misbehavior led to liquor sales being restricted on Saturday nights.

I had also not been a smoker even in college, and now on the front I relied on tobacco throughout the day. Here we faced acute shortages. Luckily, the local tribals, the Kukis, Kachins and Nagas, came to our rescue offering cheroots and bidis. Some of the women (very pretty with what I thought then were Chinese features) carried babies on their backs.

It was good to see young life, but death bore heavily on my mind that evening as I had to report on dead and wounded on both sides. The victims would have to be buried or cremated. They were sons, and husbands, and their loved ones would have to be given the tragic news, on our side at least.

A Ball at Imphal

A few weeks later, I got to attend and report on, of all things, an elegant ball. It was in honor of the visit of His Excellency Sir Andrew Clow, Governor of Assam, and Lady Clow, His Highness the Maharajah of Manipur Bodhchandra Singh hosted a dance-party in the Durbar Hall at his palace in Imphal.

It was, in its way, a graceful evening, with chandeliers illuminating the polished floors, the silver dishes laid out with care, and the music drifting out into a night pattering with monsoon rain. The Maharajah, eager to please, spared no detail. Officers of the Army and Air Force mingled with members of the Durbar and state officials, all of them maintaining the formal courtesies expected of such occasions. The British guests were amiable, if distant. A few Indian officers had been invited, though their presence, like so much else in the room, was carefully curated.

The bearers carried their trays and glasses dutifully, and in silence.

For those of us who had walked through Kanglatongbi only days before, who had watched our comrades fall in muddy trenches, the war had not ended. The Manipuris had given up their homes so that others might sleep in safety. They had grown vegetables and raised poultry for our consumption, and had brought fresh milk to our hospital tents. They had done all this willingly, even cheerfully, while risking and enduring severe repercussions for such collaboration from the Japanese.

I remember noting in an earlier dispatch that I had not seen a single beggar in the state. So it was notable that the evening's performance began with a beggar's dance. The dancers capered across the marble floor, their motions exaggerated and theatrical, while the assembled guests chuckled indulgently. The Empire had always demanded its spectacles. And the native courts, like this one, had learned how to supply them.

A slow Naga dance followed, solemn and precise. Then a boy entered, bearing two plates of fire. His gaze never wavered. His steps were light, timed to the low pulse of the drums and the flickering flame.

Finally, Pishak and little Bimla performed. Bimla could not have been more than ten, but she danced with such fierce control and lack of self-consciousness that the room was stilled. She could someday be Manipur's little art-ambassador to the world. But first we would have to be free.

Applause followed. The Governor raised his glass; the Maharajah beamed. It was one more act in the Empire's long play, carefully staged even as the theatre crumbled.

I did not write any more dispatches that night. Outside, the rain had started again.

Overall, I knew my reports were appreciated by the bosses at the PR Directorate as well as by the general public. Many of my stories had been farmed out widely, and at 30, I was getting to be well-known. It was an exciting time for me, as I discovered I enjoyed being a war correspondent, even if the battles were deeply unnerving. It was not the love of glory or even the flickering hope for Indian freedom that sustained me, but the quiet astonishment of how, under extreme conditions, character endures.

3

Shenam Saddle and Imphal Approaches[1]

April–June 1944

The Japanese drive towards Imphal encountered fierce resistance at the Shenam passes, where Allied forces fought desperately to secure the eastern approaches and maintain control of the vital Tiddim–Palel corridor.

From the plain of Kanglatongbi we headed south, climbing up into the mountains to the Shenam Saddle. The Saddle sat like a half-necklace between Manipur's Palel and Tamu in Burma. Its rocky ridgeline controlled the only passable metaled road into Imphal from the southeast. At over 5,000 feet, the Saddle did not look like a battlefield, but that was what it had become.

A young Rajput sepoy was standing beside me. He pointed at it, saying, "That ridge holds Manipur."

I knew from his look that whichever side lost the Saddle would be stranded on the wrong side of the hills, unable to reinforce or retreat. A defeat at Shenam would allow Japanese tanks and heavy artillery to destroy our key Palel airfield and then attack the town of Imphal itself. By controlling the Saddle, we could attempt to wear down the enemy, and everyone knew that meant a long, exhausting series of marathons that would sorely test our soldiers' stamina and capacity to take on additional losses. But thanks to our philosophy, we Indians are no strangers to suffering.

The road that wound up to the Saddle was a narrow thread, with winding switchbacks and blind turns. A single misjudgment would send a truck over the edge. The terrain on either side was thick with bamboo and hardwood, the kind of forest that swallowed sound and refracted light. When there was a breeze, the long bamboo tips swayed like strange mannequins. At times you could see across to the next ridge. An hour later, the fog would close in so completely that you could not see your own rifle.

Night brought the fog down to the forest floor. It blanketed everything: foxholes, boots, sentries. You learned to hold your breath when walking, to hear the crackle of twigs or the shift of cloth. The Japanese patrols knew how to move in this silence. They came close, struck quickly, and vanished again. Like our Gurkhas, they were extremely tenacious and skilled in jungle combat and fighting at close quarters. They believed surrender was dishonorable and unlike our Gurkhas, that suicide was not. Above all, what made the Japanese uniquely formidable and even terrifying, was their fanatical courage and devotion to their Emperor.[2]

The battle for the Shenam Saddle raged for two weeks, starting on April 8. Scraggy Hill and the pair known as Crete East and West became a maze of trenches, shell craters, and hand-to-hand combat. Battalions of the 20th Indian Division (1/7 Gurkha Rifles, 4/12 Frontier Force Regiment, and 3/9 Jat Regiment), backed by artillery and the 254th Indian Tank Brigade, held off night after night of Japanese infiltrations.

Our engineers from Madras laid mines and reinforced the bunkers with whatever they had. The Japanese nevertheless came in waves with their probing attacks, each meant to gather intelligence and further weaken us. Every assault tore away something from us: men, materiel, strength, and at times, territory.

The Japanese had dug themselves into the slopes. They built bunkers from logs and stone, covered in brush. We shelled them when the weather cleared, but the mist played tricks with estimates of firing range. The infantrymen had to take care of what the guns could not. They climbed, sometimes with ropes, sometimes on hands and knees, toward machine gun nests that couldn't be seen until it was too late.

For much of April and early May, fighting a mile high, our Indian troops (Rajputana Rifles, Sikh Regiments, and Madras Engineers) held the road against repeated assaults. The path forward became a muddy gauntlet of ambushes and shelling. The Japanese stayed dug in.

We sent for air support, but on some days the clouds made flying low impossible. When the sky did open up, the RAF glided over the trees, dropping crates with water, shells, rations, and boots. That last item was desperately needed as they wore out fast. Some of the drops never reached us. Overall, ammunition and supplies mattered more than food, at least on our side.

I remember the quiet, the eerie lulls between battles. Men would sit on broken crates with their socks steaming in the morning air. Some said their prayers, while others stared out into the fog. What was going through their minds was what was going through mine: the thought of our families, the battle ahead, and gathering the resolve to face the next challenge. It is intention that guides character, not some mysterious force available only to the few. And yet the same people placed in different circumstances, such as in the INA, might not have shown the same fortitude.

Whatever our thoughts, there was no denying the landscape, even in the drenching monsoon, was captivating. I waxed eloquent about the setting in my reports:

Amidst enveloping monsoon clouds and 5,200 feet above the roar of civilization, Shenam is the crowning glory of an ascents over hills where our troops are fighting the Japanese. The road is the all-weather road from Imphal to Tamu via Palel. The road twines in hair-pin bends every 100 yards and one false turn will send one's vehicle into the jungle-valleys below.

The country is beautiful and abounds in deer and gibbons. Shenam itself experiences nearly 200 inches of rain annually and the ground due to the rains is very slippery. ....The bone of contention is "Scraggy" a less higher feature in a bee-line with Malta and Gibraltar. The Japanese are entrenched on the farther side of Scraggy and our Gurkhas frequently lead attacks on them.

It is remarkable how our troops go on undisturbed by the monsoon conditions. It is quite chill here and dense clouds and mist intermittently envelop the hill-tops making it impossible for you to see a person even a couple of yards from you. Between heavy downpours a thin rain beats against your face which you may enjoy if you are on a skiing holiday on snowy slopes but not when you are fighting when it is certainly a nuisance. But our men are unperturbed and they go up and down the slopes carrying huge loads of supply and ammunition without even a propping stick to protect them from being sent rolling down from the dizzy heights. They just do it without bestowing much attention on it.

The Saddle was brutal for both humans and nature. Countless soldiers from both sides lost their lives or were maimed, along with mules and the remaining cattle that had been brought by the Japanese. The hills themselves bore the scars of war, stripped of their tree cover and burnt. Eventually, the Japanese hunkered down in their muddy bunkers which we had to clear with hand grenades.

From the bloodied slopes, the battle rolled toward the next ridge. The Brits had named it Pill, which meant it was going to be bitter.

Gurkhas advancing with Lee Tanks to clear the Japanese from Imphal–Kohima Road[3]

Pill and Liver, and a Walkover

By April 1944, the Japanese still held the high ridges above the Manipur Road. From those positions, they got to see everything: our convoys inching along the mud-slick curves, the stretcher parties hurrying along at dawn, the odd officer crouched with a Bren gun team and a field map in the open. Until those hills were taken, the road south from Imphal could not be secured. Every shell and sniper's bullet came from above.

Two of those hills bore the strange names "Pill" and "Liver." They had been assigned by British map clerks sitting in offices, and were as arbitrary as pins on a board. They were part of a string of reverse-slope defenses, where the enemy was positioned on a slope facing away from us, making it extremely difficult to observe the Japanese or to use long-range weapons to weaken them. Taking those features was tactical but crucial in denying the Japanese commanding ground and clearing the Tiddim-Tamu approaches.

On April 21, a battalion of the 9th Jat Regiment moved in. These were seasoned men who had seen action in Burma.

The attack began in the late evening. An artillery barrage opened the way, pounding Pill until it looked peeled and bare. Then the Jats advanced, bayonets fixed, grenades in hand. They climbed steadily, boots slipping in the wet earth, but the Japanese were not ready for them. The feature was taken with few casualties. I was surprised, and of course relieved.

The hill called Liver, just behind, proved harder. The Japanese had seen us coming.

Two of our companies went in, one attacking from the east, the other from the west. The western prong, made up of Punjabi Muslims, reached the lower slopes and dug in.

The eastern group was less lucky. Mortar shells landed in their column almost at once. Movement became nearly impossible; the ground was soggy and open.

The night brought more rain. It started as the usual mountain shower, and then fell in sheets, turning the hillside to clay. Japanese guns remained active, firing at intervals into the darkness. Our men stayed silent, waiting for the dawn. At first light, the fog thinned and they got to look out. The Japanese bunkers, well-camouflaged and carefully constructed, had been abandoned. Fifty Japanese lay dead in the undergrowth. Inside the dugouts, they found crates of ammunition, maps, and provisions.

It was a small gain on paper, but it altered the map decisively. From Pill and Liver, we now had a clear view of the Tiddim Road. For the fighting men, the meaning was simpler: one more ridge was now behind them instead of ahead.

Further up the road, the Dogras advancing from Imphal met no resistance at all. Skirting left into the hills, they reached the forward elements coming from Kohima without firing a shot. It was, as one officer said later, "a walkover."

Past Pill and Liver, the road curled toward Tamu, where another name awaited us: Patch.

A Captured Flag at Patch

By late April, the road from Imphal to Tamu was nearly open. Only a few Japanese positions remained. They were strongpoints dug into the slopes, blocking the highway like knots in a tightened rope. One of these was the feature known, with typical military bluntness, as Patch.

Roadblocks like Patch were tactically critical: as long as a single pillbox or strongpoint controlled the Tamu–Imphal route, the Japanese could interdict Allied resupply and reinforcement. Clearing these positions removed chokepoints, enabling the build-up of forces for later counter-attacks. Our approach combined infantry assault, local artillery, and, when weather permitted, close air support to secure the roadway.

On the morning of April 21st, two companies of the 14th Punjab Regiment were ordered forward to lift the roadblock near the 111th milestone. These were the same men who had recently taken the Mapau Ridge, and they moved now in ankle-deep mud, under steady rain, with leeches in their boots and rifles slung high to avoid water damage.

They encountered the enemy on the lower slopes of Patch. The Japanese responded immediately with a counter-attack, fast and coordinated as always. But the

Punjabis held. Twenty-five of the enemy were killed in the first exchange. Others withdrew, wounded or out of ammunition. As they disengaged, our artillery opened up. The fire was unrelenting, and it scattered their formations. Our troops surged forward, sweeping the slope. The mop-up was brutal and fast. Forty-five more Japanese were killed. Among the spoils: a battalion flag, a rare prize. The remaining enemy troops pulled back during the night, vanishing into the trees before dawn. That was the last roadblock on the Tamu Road.

One man stood out from the already courageous pack that day: Havildar Puran Singh of Sohadan, Ambala District. He had already seen action in North Africa and had won the Indian Distinguished Service Medal for his courage at El Alamein. Now, in the hills of Manipur, he saw a group of Japanese trying to haul a light machine gun into a pillbox overlooking the road. Without waiting for orders, he ran ahead alone, tommy-gun in hand, and reached the pillbox before the enemy could occupy it. In the short fight that followed, he killed one Japanese soldier and secured the position. The pillbox, empty now, stood like a dead eye overlooking the road.

By dusk the battalion flag was ours. But we still had to fight for a much greater victory to save our country. And some who helped us fight were not humans.

Of Mules and Men

Mule convoys were the silent arteries of the front. On both sides, war depended on animal transport. Many of the hills could not be navigated by wheeled vehicles. And due to the lack of forage, disease, and the difficult terrain, the Japanese lost most of their 12,000 pack horses and mules, along with 30,000 cattle used for transport and food. The results were disastrous for them.

A survey of mule companies in the 33rd Corps found that more than half the drivers has not been on leave for over 18 months, and a large number for longer periods. Nevertheless they cheerfully carried out their duties. Risaldar (Captain) Ghulam Mohideen, a Tiwana Punjabi Muslim of Mitha Tiwana, Tehsil Khush Ab, District Shahpur, and troop commander in an Animal Transport Company could only have a shave and a cup of tea before he went on another errand: he was carrying food and rations to our forward troops on the Tamu Road. Thanks to an errant guide, he was caught there between our own fire and the enemy fire. This veteran of two world wars delivered the goods all the same without any loss either to themselves or to the rations.

On the way with the rations from the supply point the Risaldar and his mule troop were lost in the jungle. The guide did not remember the way and the destination was 8 miles further away with the darkness fast setting in. As it was a dense forest they decided to camp there for the night. The guide was made prisoner for misleading them. The Risaldar chose for his camp a nullah a little away from the jungle. When he had moved 15 yards in the nullah, he saw cigarette sparks at a distance. Then he saw movements in the grass. Scenting that it was the enemy he decided to hurry away from them with his precious cargo. As he was turning back the enemy fired at his company with mortar, Bren and other guns. Covering his animals with bayonets in case of attack he proceeded further when he found that his company was being fired at even from the front. These were our own troops to whom he was carrying supplies but who mistook him and his men for the enemy because they were coming from the direction of the enemy positions!

Caught between two fires, the Risaldar slowly extricated his company away from the area of fire but 10 mule-loads of ration fell off in the confusion. He delivered the rest of the rations to the unit and went back to fetch the fallen rations which he collected and delivered to another unit as per schedule. On his way back he passed through the same nullah the next morning where he rescued two of his mules which had fallen the previous night. He found that the Japanese had disappeared from there.

Risaldar Ghulam Mohideen has 25 years' experience and served in the last war with the Baluch Horse (37 Lancers) in Persia, France and Afghanistan and later in Wazirstan with the 41 Camel Transport Company.

His Commanding Officer only said, "The animals know him. He knows them too." No more was added when Sharif returned with the two mules the next morning.

In the confusion of supply drops and slit trenches, a mule was often more than transport.

"Little Mule, Little man, little feet" is the song in a mule company on the road to Tamu. The mule known as "China" escaped from Burma and attached himself to a Naga pony and has never left him. He is only about nine hands in height and both he and his inseparable friend were caught by a muleteer in the thick jungles on the border of Burma. The muleteer himself is only four feet in height but army boots do not have the size to suit his little foot.

Sher Zeman's Last Stand

Courage wore many faces. Sometimes it was a mule driver, sometimes a gunner, sometimes a tankman. Where the terrain allowed it, tanks and armored vehicles provided mobile firepower. However, tracks and mines could immobilize crews and expose them to concentrated mortar and infantry anti-tank action.

Sher Zeman of an Indian Tank Brigade and of village Mitial, Campbellpur district, was on the Ukhrul Road when his tank came under heavy mortar and small arms fire from the enemy. They managed to blow a track off the tank. Both his legs were smashed by a heavy mortar which came through the plate right above his knee. The rest of the crew evacuated the tank and put out the flames with the small fire extinguisher and earth. During this time Sher Zaman, in spite of his desperate condition and unaided, provided covering fire for them. He heroically managed to fire two bursts from the 37 mm anti-tank gun and several from the co-axial Browning machine gun, which the rest of the crew viewed as a miracle.

After the fire had been put out, the enemy fire became intense, and the crew were compelled to take cover in a nullah. Sher Zaman climbed out of the tank and expired on the ground near it a few minutes later.

To save one's tank is one of the highest codes of honor in any tank regiment. Sher Zeman was buried near the wreck, without any kind of memorial, but his sacrifice is remembered.

Fruit Baskets on Scraggy

Beyond the ridge where Sher Zeman fell, other hills rose again: Scraggy, Malta, and Gibraltar, names that sounded like Europe transplanted into Asia's green heart. Scraggy sat in a bee-line with Malta and Gibraltar, to the east of the mountain-village of Shenma on the Palel-Tamu Road. Together with its neighbouring hill features, it was a locus of sustained infantry fighting. Capturing those summits would mean breaking the Japanese line of communication and enable broader movement along the Palel–Tamu Road.

The Japanese were entrenched on the farther side of Scraggy from whose top one could command a complete view of the entire topography to the east. Our Gurkhas and other units frequently led small-scale raids and offensive patrols on the Japanese positions there, clearing bunkers with grenades. The object was to kill as many Japanese as possible and secure information regarding their positions.

Men of the Tenth Gurkha Rifles clearing enemy positions on Scraggy, April 1944[4]

As I stood on the top of Malta and watched the Gurkhas practice their craft, the serene atmosphere was disturbed by an occasional enemy 75 mm, one of which fell 20 yards behind me as I was returning.

One night, Naik Narbahadur Gurung and his comrade Naik Mahabir Pun of the 5th Gurkhas crept behind enemy lines and dropped grenades into the sleeping quarters of about 40 Japanese. At least 10 Japanese were killed. They returned unscathed.

On 17/18 June night, Naik Narbahadur Gurung in command and Naik Mahabir Pun as second in command, moving round the western flank of Scraggy worked their way up to the extreme north of the hill. Keeping an LMG behind with one of the Gurkhas to attract the enemy fire the two Naiks stealthily crept up to the skyline and behind the enemy sentry post. As they were moving further they heard snores from a bunker. They then dropped two grenades through it. Immediately cries of terror and pain rent the air. One Japanese who ran out of the bunker was hit by a grenade. In the confusion and in the thick darkness of the night more Japanese came out of their bunkers and began to run helter-skelter in terror. The noise was terrific. Those who went into the slit trenches were hit by more than a dozen grenades thrown by the Naiks, killing at least 10 enemy.

At the time, I did not question the killing of sleeping or unarmed men. Once, at Chothe in the Bishenpur area, an unarmed Japanese approached our post from the south with both his hands in the air. Losing his nerve at the last moment, he tried to run away but was shot and killed by our Gurkha troops. It did not strike us as odd, and was perhaps even amusing. Such is the psychological mindset of warriors in battle.

In another phase of the Scraggy assault, Naiks Ajirath Rai and Shyamdal Rai hailing from East Nepal, crept forward under heavy fire.

Naik Ajirath Rai of the 10th Gurkhas was section commander of a platoon attacking the hill from one side, when his section was held up by fire from a large bunker. Taking one man with him, he went forward and leaning over the top of the bunker threw into it three grenades. As he could still hear the enemy inside, he swung into the entrance and was met by Japanese with an LMG. Seizing the LMG with one hand he shot the Japanese with the other. His platoon suffered heavy casualties and along with another were the only NCOs left. Taking command of the platoon, he charged to the crest of the hill and was fired on from a bunker they had passed. Going up to the bunker alone with a home-made flame thrower, he and his fellow Naik Shyamdal Rai lobbed several grenades into a fortified machine gun post inserted into the entrance. Three Japanese who ran out were dealt with.

Naik Shyamdal Rai, finding his platoon held up, crawled forward with his haversack full of grenades. With complete disregard to his own safety, he in turn stalked five different enemy bunkers and throwing grenades into them, enabled his platoon to attack and capture the objective.

"It was like distributing fruits from a basket," remarked one of his officers to me.

Havildar Dhan Singh, Lance–Havildar Dhan Bahadur Gurung and Rifleman Lal Bahadur Rai of the 10th Gurkha Rifles resting after the capture of Scraggy, 1944[5]

The sign *Welcome to Gilliam Manor* at the entrance to a Regimental Aid Post at the foot of Malta was rather intriguing. I found that it was entirely due to the fame that Cairo-born Neil Gilliam of a Field Ambulance earned on these dizzy heights. During an enemy attack on our positions on Scraggy, he hurried forward to the frontline to evacuate the wounded. When communication between our most forward troops and our rear HQ failed, he acted as a jeep dispatch rider between them, all under the heaviest fire from the enemy. The wooden board has been put up by his admirers in the Field Ambulance.

The battle for Scraggy was fought over several months till July 24 when a battalion of the 10th Gurkha Regiment finally captured it after an intense grenade battle lasting for nearly four hours. This opened our line of communication to the forward troops of the 23rd Indian Division under Major-General Ouvry Roberts who had reached Tengnoupal and Sibong, encircling the forward troops of the enemy.

Abandoned Japanese Equipment on Malta as seen from Scraggy, 1944[6]

What remained on Scraggy after the battle were stinking dead bodies of the enemy, large quantities of ammunition and weapons, rations and equipment and records containing valuable information. Scraggy itself was bald, most of its trees having been razed to the ground with vast bomb-craters and pot-holes yawning out in the pouring rain.

While Scraggy burned in the south, another ridge farther north had been under siege with ferocious close-up combat.

Combat on Kohima's Garrison Hill

The Battle of Kohima began on April 4 with a fierce 14-day siege. An Allied garrison (Assam Regiment, 4th Battalion Royal West Kent Regiment, and attached units) was encircled on Kohima Ridge by the far superior Japanese 31st Division. The defenders fought tenaciously over a tiny perimeter, including the famous close-quarters combat around the Deputy Commissioner's tennis court on Garrison Hill, until the siege was relieved on April 18 by the arrival of the British 2nd Division. The Allied counter-offensive began immediately, but it took a month to dislodge the dogged Japanese from the heights, after which they were hunted down. The Battle finally ended on June 22 when Allied forces from Kohima and Imphal linked up at Milestone 109.

The siege of Kohima revealed how modern war, despite its artillery and air power, could collapse into the brutal intimacy of the olden days. Every yard was contested with guns, grenades, bayonets, and raw resolve. On the knife-edged slopes farther south, the fighting bore the same grim proximity, men confronting each other to death.

The Art of Close Combat

Close combat with bayonets was essential in reverse-slope attacks under poor visibility. This older style of warfare would have been hopeless without the use of hand-grenades. And in confrontations involving direct attacks, attempting surprise but often failing, soldiers from opposite sides often ended up facing each other a few yards away.

May 24th witnessed a gallant young Sikh officer leading the Rajputs in a bayonet attack on the strong Japanese position of Shehnam on Palel Road. Lieutenant Daljit Singh Randhawa, 6th Rajputana Rifles, of Chak No. 66/12L, district Montgomery (near Toba Tek Singh), was in the forefront of a bayonet attack on a knife-edged ridge where the Japanese were entrenched. The enemy were concentrating fire from their machine gun posts on the higher slopes of the ridge.

The Rajputs who had to climb the slope suffered early casualties, but Lieutenant Daljit Singh undaunted went ahead and when within a couple of yards from an enemy LMG post threw two hand grenades into it which accounted for two Japanese. All the while he was covered by LMG fire from another section of the Rajputs from behind. Four Japanese who came from his right to close in on him were pinned down by the Rajput LMG and killed. Very far ahead of his men, he advanced further.

The next few moments were dramatic. He and a Japanese were facing each other only a few yards between them. The enemy soldier's eyes were gleaming, and they had a full measure of each other from top to toe.

"It was a tense moment," said Lieutenant Daljit Singh, describing the incident to me in the hospital where he was recovering from his wounds. "The Japanese beckoned to me with his finger but I said 'Tairo' (Wait). The next thing I did instinctively was to throw my remaining two hand grenades at him. I could not see the result as I was injured immediately but I am sure I did not miss the mark."

While having his field dressing, Lieutenant Daljit Singh requested his Commanding Officer to send him out again to have another crack at the Japanese but it was not granted. However his men cleared the position of the enemy and held it. In addition to large enemy casualties, part of the booty were two Japanese LMGs.

Colonel Daljit Singh Randhawa in later life

Daljit Singh was decorated the very next year with the Military Cross for his exploits here. At 24, he was the youngest to be given that award.*

Valor of this sort can arise in every soldier. It is triggered by extreme circumstances, caring nothing for clan, creed, or doubt.

Near Bishenpur, Jemadar (Second Lieutenant) Sattar Khan led a bayonet charge through mist and mortar fire.

Ahead of his men in a bayonet charge on a strongly-held enemy position, Jemadar Sattar Khan, 12th Frontier Force Rifles, of village Shakrdhara, district Kohat, NWFP, engaged a Japanese officer in a hand-to-hand scuffle.

It was a misty day when a company of the 12th Frontier Force Rifles led a bayonet-charge on a steep and barren hill northwest of Bishenpur. Though there was our artillery barrage prior to that, because of the poor visibility our attack completely surprised the enemy, who strongly entrenched on its crest and further slopes. When our company was quite close the enemy started firing their mortars and shells. Undeterred, the Jemadar

---

*In 1947, at the first Independence Day Parade in Delhi, Daljit Singh served as the parade commander. He later became a colonel. He came from a family that has served in the military for more than seven generations and died in Hoshiarpur at the age of 96.

advanced ahead of his company and was the first to reach the crest, where he engaged a Japanese officer in close combat. Unable to break free from the grip of this Viceroy's Commissioned Officer (previously known as a "native officer"), the enemy soldier detonated one of his own grenades, killing both.

Only two weeks earlier Jemadar Sattar Khan while on patrol had killed 12 Japanese and captured 1 enemy LMG. The Japanese lost the position but counter-attacked the same night when they came within 3 yards of our forward line on the crest but were driven off by our grenades. The morning count showed 32 Japanese dead.

Sattar Khan's grave was shallow, without a marker, near the place he fell. His family in NWFP would be notified in due course, and it would be left to them to mourn. He had friends in his regiment who would undoubtedly miss him, but I never heard any of them say anything further about him. Civilians have the luxury of mourning, but grief softens the soul, and in wartime too much softening can be deadly.

Night Ambush and a Daring Rescue

For every hill we stormed, another road had to be cleared. The Tiddim and Tamu roads were under nightly threat. Japanese units laid mines, blocked paths with trees and boulders, and ambushed convoys, especially at night. Allied troops had to run clearing operations under fire so that forward troops would not be starved of ammunition or reinforcements.

Lieutenant Harpratap Singh, of the 45th Cavalry Regiment (the first Indian tank regiment to go into action in this theatre of war) hailed from Daudpur, Ludhiana district. He was leading a troop of tanks to clear a road-block on the Tiddim Road. Backed by Gurkha infantry support, they managed to advance but were attacked by entrenched enemy forces. His troop came under heavy machine gun and mortar fire.

Harpratap brought down the enemy snipers in the trees and destroyed an enemy bunker. Some of the Japanese who came close to his tank to dislocate the vision instruments were killed and their attempts to use anti-tank weapons were foiled. Subsequently, while withdrawing under orders because of nightfall, he and his troop were ambushed by a party of the enemy at a curve further down the road. They still managed to kill 15 Japanese and, under heavy fire from the enemy, rescued 2 wounded Gurkhas who were lying right across the road.

When his troop ventured out again the next day on the road, the enemy had disappeared but had laid trees and other obstructions and mines on the road which they cleared to enable our supply convoy to pass. They then relieved the troops who had been held up by this road-block.

Clearing road-blocks is not associated with glory, and in civilian life this is viewed as a traffic function. However, in war, what might seem mundane can be of immense consequence, requiring acts of extreme bravery. Lieutenant Harpratap Singh did well, and deserves to be remembered.

Curds and Other Cure-Alls

Already, within two months, the battle to save India had been terribly costly. The casualties would in fact have been much higher if not for the extraordinary dedication and work ethic of our medical staff, who had to fight a different kind of battle, one aimed at preserving life at all costs. As the front lines shifted and air and land evacuation routes changed, the staff had to adapt to floods, monsoon, and limited evacuation routes.

Wading through waist-deep water, Captain S.V. Krishniah, Indian Army Medical Corps, of Kovvur, West Godavari district, made his daily round of visits to patients' beds in a hospital on the Imphal front. The space between the different wards had been flooded by the monsoon rains. The next two days the water rose to about 15 feet.

The doctor, undeterred, made his rounds on assault boats and rafts built with old petrol drums as floats. It was yet another instance of *jugaad* to the rescue.

Meanwhile the Anti-Malaria unit of the hospital whose work of killing the mosquito larvae had been taken over by the floods, got busy and built a temporary bridge. Serious cases for admission were brought in on assault boats and discharge cases comfortably sailed on the rafts. The hospital routine went on as usual during the time the floods lasted. Immediate operations were carried out on incoming patients, daily doses of medicine and diet were not missed and some officers even had their usual gramophone records played for them.

Dr. Julu is a familiar figure in a Casualty Clearing Section on the Imphal front. "Dr. Julu" is short for Captain K.J. Somayajulu, Indian Army Medical Corps, of Vizianagaram. He was previously practicing medicine in Jeypore, Orissa. He has been given the additional status of "Distinguished Service Order (D.S.O.)" by the troops; it stands for "Dahi (Curds), Supplying Officer." He prepares curds daily for his patients, sometimes from tinned milk. In abdominal and other surgical cases his curds are given to Indian patients on the recommendation of the Surgical specialist. Dr. Julu is enthusiastic about introducing in his hospital a cup of buttermilk instead of tea.

Nursing Indian and British troops at a half-way house near Kohima are two charging Naga cousins, Miss Kesovole Angami (22 years) and Miss Vikole Angami (18 years). They do the dressings and dispense the medicines besides helping the medical officer in the operations. The older lady is a trained nurse while the younger is an enthusiastic beginner. They both speak fluent Hindustani. Coming from the village of Jakhoma, only a few miles away, their presence attracts a large number of Nagas seeking medical relief for whose treatment the army has provided special facilities.

Showing symptoms of an acute stage of kidney inflammation or nephritis, a 12-year-old Naga girl was brought in one evening by the villagers to a hospital near Kohima while there was fierce fighting ongoing. Assisting an Indian medical officer were four British servicemen. The Army has provided excellent facilities for rendering medical relief to the friendly Nagas who are the local scouts and terrain experts, as well as fearsome warriors indispensable to our victory there. The Indian doctor knew it was a battle against death given the patient's condition but with the encouragement of the servicemen he thought he might yet save her life. Every hour of the night was marked with an injection, until things began to improve early in the morning. As a token of their gratitude, the Nagas from the girl's village invited the doctor and the servicemen to a party. The lucky invitees were: Lieutenant Chandra Mohan Patnaik, Indian Army Medical Corps; Regimental Sergeant Major George Todd, of Landseer Road, Ipswich, Suffolk; Sub-conductor Herbert Haywood of 23, Laurel Road, Dudley, Worcestershire; Battery Sergeant Major Victor Peal of 25, Grange Rd, Southall, Middlesex; and Sergeant Walter Graves of 17, Drake Rd, Fazakerley, Liverpool.

Wherever nurses were present, they were greatly appreciated by the troops. This was of course due to their caring so well for the sick and wounded, but also because amid the hardships of war, the soldiers deeply missed the warmth of human connection and care. The nurses' presence and caring actions did wonders for everyone's morale.*

---

*As an officer in General Gracey's Twentieth Indian Division observed: "The employment of female nursing officers not only in the Casualty Clearing Stations but in certain circumstances at MS level has been shown to be not only possible and reasonably safe but, in fact, very desirable. Apart from the immeasurably enhanced efficiency noticeable whenever women take charge of patients, the effect on morale is always marked. It may be remarked that in certain quarters the employment of women in such circumstances was viewed with misgiving. The reaction of the nurses themselves has always been one of ultra enthusiasm." As confirmed in the Gracey Collection at the Liddell Hart Centre for Military Archives.

In the midst of unspeakable destruction and suffering, the touch, care, and human connection was what healed most, even more than the salves and bandages and medical interventions.

Outside the wards, the engines kept running. The war still needed its drivers.

Drivers Under Fire

On the Palel–Tamu approaches, drivers ran day-and-night convoys over hairpin, mine-strewn roads. Saving vehicles and payloads under fire was often the difference between holding a forward position and collapse. Working right up to the front on the Tiddim Road, eight drivers of a General Purpose Transport company of the Royal Indian Army Service Corps saved all their vehicles from the enemy who were close on their heels even though their tires were flat and their hydraulic brakes refused to work because of the damage due to enemy shelling.

Under the command of Lieutenant C.B. Karumbayya of Sidapur, Coorg, and formerly of the Nizam State Railways, Secunderabad, these men showed devotion to duty removing as many vehicles as possible when one of our positions was being evacuated owing to heavy artillery and mortar fire from the enemy. It was a dark night and during a lull in the enemy firing these drivers started their vehicles but the fire opened up again as soon as the sound of starting reached the enemy. Due to shelling the tires then ran flat, the hydraulic brakes refused to function and the engines would not start. Remaining cool and calm they succeeded in rescuing all the vehicles, leaving none behind.

The MTS (Motor Transport Service) drivers were: Naik Mahadev Shivte of Bhaing, Satara District; Lance Naik Khader Hussain Khan of Chilkalguda, Secunderabad; Sepoy K. Bab Jahn of Big Masjeed St., Wallajapet, North Arcot district; Sepoy Basweni Mekalki of Hukeri, Belgaon district; Sepoy Hussain Khan Pathan of Upali Burj, Bijapur district; Sepoy Gurpadappa Murbagi of Murbagi, Bijapur district; and Sepoy Vemanari of Parakondlapalli, Anantapur district.

More strange was the adventure of their companion Naik J. Jesuratnam of Thandalam, Chingleput district. During the enemy shelling, his radiator was incapacitated. Having previously seen a damaged vehicle 5 miles behind on the road toward the enemy, he walked back alone and personally removed the radiator from the damaged vehicle. He ran back with it to fit it to his own vehicle which he drove back to safety.

"I was really worried and nearly gave him up for lost when he suddenly turned up with a spare radiator," his

Commanding Officer said to me. "He was smiling, and we understood immediately that he had saved his vehicle and the ammunition in it."

Feeding our troops while we pushed the Japanese to Tamu was one of the oldest General Purpose Transport companies in this area. This Royal Indian Army Service Corps (RIASC) unit carried rations, petrol and ammunition to our most forward troops along the Tamu Road with its hair-pin bends, steep slopes and muddy and slushy pits. A single slip could send a truck plunging into the gorge. Naturally, the drivers didn't speak of such matters; their focus was on keeping the wheels turning.

They have been on the road night and day for the last 14 days with an average of nearly 130 vehicles a day. Mines are the nightmare of drivers on this road and the feeding tracks, and many a soldier was maimed or killed en route.

Recently Sepoy Mahmud Khan of village Kheda Afghani, district Saharanpur, a jeep driver in this company, was running his jeep-ambulance down the Sita track with two seriously-wounded and four walking wounded when it was blown up by a land-mine left by the retreating Japanese. Despite enemy sniping, the sepoy moved the injured soldiers to cover and, after placing them in the care of a muleteer, ran 3 miles to bring back another ambulance. His courage, prompt response, and decisive action saved the lives of the seriously wounded men.

Every load delivered, every engine saved, was another day the line held. And in the trenches ahead, men waited for word from the outside world.

World News in the Trenches

Late in the evening on June 6, Major R.A. Anthony of Berkhamstead, England, heard the news of the opening of the Second Front in Europe while sitting in a water-logged slit trench on Squeak Hill near the Manipur Road. With leeches clinging to his skin, cradling the telephone near his ear, he kept shouting out what he could hear on the phone call from his battalion HQ. The Allies had launched a vast seaborne attack on the beaches of Normandy.

There was a snippet of General "Ike" Eisenhower's address to the troops. His calm, plainspoken American voice came on.

"The eyes of the world are upon you. … In company with our brave Allies and brothers-in-arms on other Fronts, you will bring about the destruction of the German war machine, the elimination of Nazi tyranny over the oppressed peoples of Europe, and security for ourselves in a free world."

It was surreal to hear of earth-shaking events from halfway across the world come through a crackling wire while we were ensconced knee-deep in mud. The men were happy that Jerry might finally be getting his comeuppance. But some of us also knew that the fight there would be hard, with thousands sacrificed on those beaches in full sight of German gun batteries.

Meanwhile, life for us was not going to change much. The Japanese would fight even more fiercely. But the thought of our brothers-in-arms battling valiantly there gave us hope.

Major Anthony looked weary as he put back the telephone. He had been through hell himself. He had been commanding a company of the 14th Punjab Regiment who were engaged in driving the Japanese from the Road. They were sent behind the enemy lines to cut their lines of communication. After a hard journey in torrents of rain and slippery terrain with the valley below ready to receive any unfortunate, he and his company of Punjabi Muslims captured Squeak Hill, located between two enemy positions. Under constant sniping by day and counter-attacks at night they spent the next three days in slit trenches with water to nearly a foot's height. This sort of accommodation in soaking clothes made them suffer severely from cramps. Their rations were short but the leeches had plenty, having developed a taste for fighting blood. The soldiers' living space grew increasingly restricted owing to the landslides caused by the heavy rains. The mud from the walls of the trenches were gradually burying them. They survived, nevertheless, proving that there are few limits to human endurance.

I too was surprised at my own capacity to take on hardship. Perhaps that is all that war teaches the soldier, through all its horror: that he can endure almost anything, if he survives. And that his final fate is not in his hands.

As a war correspondent, I also discovered that a man's courage stems from relentless, uncelebrated physical and mental labors. Whether he is hauling ammunition up rain-slicked slopes, threading narrow, mud-choked roads, tending the wounded through flooded wards, or coaxing stalled vehicles back to life under fire, or making split-second decisions, he endures because the line must hold, because someone has to keep the wheels turning, the animals moving, the rations coming, the food cooked, the guns and grenades and tanks and knives at hand and ready to strike.

Death and the enemy linger in every shell crater, in the fog-shrouded bends of the road, in waving bamboo thickets, a presence half-seen, watching, ready to destroy. The hills, the mud, the relentless monsoon rains bear down with the same indifference, testing him ceaselessly; yet it is in his stubborn persistence in the presence of dread, in the careful attention to duty and to one another amid carnage, that courage is forged, moment by moment.

4

Ukhrul–Palel Ridge Positions[1]

May–September 1944

Allied advances through the Ukhrul highlands sever Japanese lines of withdrawal, driving them off the ridge systems that dominate the routes into the Imphal and Kabaw valleys.

By May 1944, the war along the Burma–India border had reached its breaking point. The Japanese U-Go offensive had driven deep toward Imphal and Kohima, but starvation, monsoon rains, and unyielding defense were beginning to turn the tide. On the Imphal front, Indian units fought in scattered hill posts and jungle tracks, holding ground inch by inch as the Allies prepared their counter-stroke. Each ridge taken or held was part of a larger struggle that, by June, would push the enemy back toward the Chindwin and reopen the road to Kohima.

The story of Imphal was not a single clash but a chain of struggles, of hill posts held through sleepless nights, of ambushes in jungle rain, of cooks who became fighters, and of porters who labored through mud and shellfire. In these encounters, the Indian Army revealed its many faces: the ferocity of the Sikhs, the stealth of the Gurkhas, the steadfast defense of the Frontier Force, the faith of the Rajputs and Pathans, and the quiet endurance of the Madrasis and Pioneers who kept the front alive.

Manipur was won back by brilliant planning and discipline, as well as armaments and logistics. Most of all, it was achieved by the moral stamina of an extremely diverse but united Indian Army. Among the countless acts of courage on the Imphal front, the Rajendra Sikhs distinguished themselves with a feat that would echo through the campaign.

The Offensive Spirit

Unique in their tactics, the Rajendra Sikhs, a battalion of the 1st Patiala Regiment, managed to strike terror in the hearts of Japanese on the Imphal front. Their objective was a hill-feature near Palel and south-east of Litang, a good observation-point nearly 4,600 feet high and 15 miles across from where they were. The 80-strong enemy were well dug-in on this steep height isolated from all directions. At 10 o'clock during the day, Naik Mohender Singh, 11 years with the battalion and an experienced soldier, went with another Naik and silently crept into the enemy positions. Staying there for four hours he heard them talk and after gauging their defenses returned to his HQ. He then volunteered to take a section into the midst of the enemy.

The same evening one of their companies went around to sit behind the enemy line of communication until the appointed time. Another company was sent at four in the morning to approach the enemy position from the north but still remained in hiding till the signal was given to attack. When the OK was heard from both companies before half past six, the Naik and his section daringly crept right into the enemy position and lay in wait there. Half an hour later, our company coming from the north started a vigorous attack and the enemy opened fire.

At that point, the Naik and his section shouted *Sat Sri Akaal (Truth is Timeless)* from the center of the enemy position. It was followed by the same war cry by our attacking company. The enemy was confused, stopped fire and dispersed immediately, leaving the feature to us. We captured the position without any casualties on our side.

One Japanese was killed and many wounded. The enemy did not retreat by his supply route, where he would have been attacked, but simply scattered away into the bamboo groves on the hillside.

After the bold and fearless storming of the hill near Palel, the battle moved into darkness and silence. Patrols from the 10th Gurkhas had been pushing along the Tamu Road, in small stealthy raiding teams that would ruthlessly achieve their goals. Their fighting styles could not be more different. The Sikhs were famed for aggressive frontal assaults and their steadfastness in trench and hill fighting with bayonets, often invoking their warrior creed of *Dharam Yudh*, the righteous war. The Gurkhas, while no less brave, were light-footed, superb infantrymen, well-suited to combat in this rough terrain. They specialized in skillful field craft, sudden maneuvering, and terrifying close-quarters combat with their khukris.

The Green Diamond was the battle sign of the 10th Gurkhas. Leading a three-man reconnaissance patrol in torrential rains on a dark night without the moon, Naik Siriman Sunwar, a Gurkha of East Nepal, laid a successful ambush on a Japanese convoy on the Tamu Road behind the enemy lines. It was until then the farthest position that any of our patrols had reached on this road. Working their way across waist-deep nullahs of running water, the patrol penetrated behind the enemy lines and laid up two nights running at Milestone 44 on the Tamu Road. On the second night (June 14) they ambushed an empty Japanese convoy of five trucks.

As the leading lorry came level with him the Naik opened fire at close range with his tommy gun and killed both the driver and the man sitting close to him. The other two Gurkha riflemen followed suit and opened fire on the second and third lorries and killed both the drivers. As more Japanese jumped out of the lorries, the Gurkhas lobbed more grenades.

The Gurkhas' fearless feats showed that small, precise actions could shape the battle in our favor. However, to repel invaders, defense mattered just as much as attack. Raiding success meant little unless our line held. On a hill aptly named Sausage by the Brits, a lone post was exemplary in that regard, enduring four repeated assaults in a single night.

The Unyielding Defence

Beating off four successive heavy enemy attacks in one night, a unit of the 13th Frontier Force Rifles defending 4,000-foot Sausage on the road to Ukhrul has earned hearty congratulations from the Corps Commander. A company under Major James Braine Watson of 123, Bridge Road, East Molesey, Surrey, were defending this position which lies nearly 5 miles to the north-east of Yaingangpokpi and nearly 17 from Imphal. The night of June 24–25 was completely dark when at about seven-thirty in the evening the Japanese put in their first attack preceded by heavy 4-inch mortar barrage and 75 mm guns. Two companies of the enemy attacked our bunkers with LMGs, grenades and mortars to which we replied with LMGs and mortars. Beaten back, they withdrew about 200 yards, in all suffering nearly 20 casualties.

In another three hours, the enemy attacked again with the usual barrage but yelling and shouting incomprehensible slogans. After quarter of an hour's fighting, they were beaten once again. Meanwhile they collected their dead. After four hours, they put in the third attack when a party of about 15 Japanese broke into our perimeter through the wire. Two Japanese were killed near one of our mortar positions and three more who approached our company HQ were shot down. The rest of the Japanese fled, but they were nothing if not persistent. Two hours later, for the fourth time, they attacked our position and did not press it in strength because they had suffered too much depletion in their numbers. In a fight lasting for about 15 minutes our troops rushed at them with tommy-guns and bayonets and inflicted heavy casualties. They withdrew with a total of 110 casualties.

By this time, yet another Japanese company was digging in on the north side of Sausage only 75 yards away from our wire. During the day there was heavy sniping and exchange of mortar. At ten in the morning a couple of platoons of Japanese crept into within 400 yards of our position and started shelling us with mortars. Within 10 minutes our guns were ranged on them and knocked them off.

Subedar (Captain) Abdul Rauf of village Shadi Khel, District Kohat in NWFP, was second in command during these attacks when he showed complete disregard for his own personal safety and exposed himself to enemy fire as he went round encouraging his men.

"I told them to think of the Japanese as rabid village dogs," he said. "And they treated them accordingly. The Japanese were in fact like madmen. One of them was clinging to one of our mortars with a tight hold when I had to shoot him down. Another officer of theirs was running like a chicken with its head cut off until I took him down too."

The men of this company look like real jungle inhabitants in their jungle caps and they have to their credit yet another victory of one of its guerilla platoons over the Japanese. It was only about a fortnight ago at Thawai, 5 miles to the west of Yaingangpokpi, when they attacked and inflicted large casualties on a company of the enemy. Major Watson and Subedar Abdul Rauf were leading the guerilla platoon.

As June rains thickened, the enemy became weaker and the war was beginning to turn. Our work shifted to stealth and observation. Patrols began probing outward, scouts mapping the enemy's positions for quick attacks and mop-ups. Men risked the open ground to read the enemy's next move.

Tea Ceremonies

Carrying out a daring daylight reccy right in the heart of enemy positions, Naik Dilbarar Singh, a Jat Sikh of village Kaleke, Patiala State, brought back valuable information regarding enemy dispositions which enabled us to capture the village of Sirukhong in the Iril Valley in the middle of June.

A Naik of the 12th Frontier Force Regiment, Dilbarar was sent forward to recce the village in daytime and seeing that he could not take the whole of his section, crept forward alone past the enemy sentries and forward posts. Moving past sentries and scrub, he found a church and eased open a wooden window. Inside, a group of Japanese soldiers sat talking over their tea.

Dilbarar dropped two grenades through the opening and withdrew without waiting to confirm the results. He returned with a sketch held in memory: positions, footpaths, the number of guards. It was enough. The village was taken that evening.

Sepoy Dinaram, a Dogra Rajput of village Ladha, district Udhampur, Punjab, was with his 12th Frontier Force platoon when it was heavily attacked by the enemy at Chepu. Noticing a Jap LMG causing heavy casualties, he rushed at it from a distance of 20 yards. The Japanese LMG and its crew were silenced. On his way back, he spotted a sniper perched in a tree and shot him, though not before being hit himself. Severely wounded, he returned to find his platoon nearly out of ammunition. He made three trips to the depot under continuous fire. After being treated for blood loss, he boiled tea and carried it, cup by cup, to serve his section.

While Dilbarar Singh and Dinaram showed exemplary courage, that virtue was not of course confined to soldiers. Even those whose duty seemed far from battle would find themselves stepping into the fight, showing that heroism could appear in the most unexpected forms.

Cooking for a Fight

Mohamed Sharif, a Pathan of Dheri Kahal, district Hazara, NWFP, was a young cook in a battalion of the 6th Rajputana Rifles. We were at Lone Tree Hill battling the enemy. The Japanese were about two companies strong and having arrived right behind our positions at Shenam, had established themselves on this hill about 4 miles to the west which was overlooking our LOC from Palel. For our advance up the road it was imperative that the Japanese should be ousted from this hill. Scraggy, the hill next door, had already been liberated by the Gurkhas. Lone Tree was left as the Rajput's cake.

Seeing all the patrons from the mess tent heading off to battle, Sharif became restless and told me he was going to his commanding officer to request a crack at the Japanese, and asked if I would accompany him. On meeting the Commanding Officer (CO), he simply said, "I am always restless when my battalion is fighting and I would like to fight instead of cooking."

His CO quickly replied: "We cannot afford to lose a good cook like you."

I still had half a morsel of chapatti and curry in my mouth and managed to remain silent. Sharif looked crestfallen.

That was not the end of the story. On the sly, he and another orderly secured rifles and ammunition and went up toward the crest of the hill and joined the fighting. Their absence was noticed at the HQ and they were given up for missing. Six hours later, to everyone's surprise, he returned alone. He was carrying a Japanese ammunition pouch.

The next morning, he whipped off again without permission when the whole area was infested with enemy snipers, and brought back a 11-inch long Japanese sword which he displayed proudly to me.

The CO took no action against him. Some rules, like uniforms, wear thin under fire.

The front never stayed quiet for long. Even as Sharif returned to his kitchen, hunger was tightening its grip on the enemy. While our food supplies were plentiful, the enemy had no such bounty. One Japanese soldier was eating grass from his mess tin when he was disturbed by Havildar Baggi Ram, 13th Frontier Force Rifles, of village Chadial, tehsil Palanpur, district Kangra. The Japanese soldier was asked to surrender and he replied with a grenade that only wounded himself. The Havildar advanced but the enemy threw another grenade at him which Baggi Ram dodged. A quick stab from the Havildar's bayonet put an end to that hunger.

While the enemy clawed at empty rations, our soldiers drew strength from their traditions as they readied themselves for the clash to come. Across the hills, the Rajputs steeled for a strike, their lips ready with a battle cry that bound them to their ancestors.

The Call to Faith and Action

At dusk on July 23rd, two platoons of the 6th Rajputana Rifles began their ascent toward Lone Tree Hill. It was dense with cover and slick with monsoon rain. Each step forward meant slipping, then regaining balance, then moving again.

The enemy held the top, dug in and watching. Subedar Sardar Khan of Bharot village, Gujrat district, led the left flank. The gap to the Japanese line was 30 yards. Grenades cleared the first cover. His men followed as he shouted the old Rajput battle cry *Raja Ramchandraji ki Jai* (*Glory to Lord Rama*). Small arms fire came in bursts. A cup discharger arced low from the far slope.

One grenade struck him directly. Sardar Khan was killed where the crest began to break. His war cry was the last words I heard from him, and I can think of no better final words.

The men did not stop, and when they reached the top, they held it. When the enemy positions were cleared, over 150 Japanese were found dead in the trenches; more were pulled away by their retreating lines. Unwanted equipment was left behind in crates and dugouts, the ugly detritus of war.

Lone Tree Hill fell after days of savage fighting, but the battleline did not rest. Even as the Rajputs held their hard-won crest, fresh attacks flared along the Ukhrul Road.

Faith took many tongues but spoke with one meaning: unyielding courage. On another ridge, men of the Frontier Force Regiment tried their utmost to hold on. The Rajputs' cry to Rama was replaced here by a bold Pathan's call to Haider.

A battalion of the 12th Frontier Force Regiment held a ridge overlooking the Japanese positions near Chepu, west of Milestone 28 on the Ukhrul Road. During the night, a larger enemy force attacked. The company commander was killed. So was the Commanding Officer.

At dawn, Subedar Kagir Khan of Girdi village, Campbellpur district, took command. He gathered what remained of the company and led them up the hill. The ground was slick, the tree cover patchy. The bayonet charge lasted 20 minutes. No orders were shouted; just a few clipped curses, and then a cry: *Maro! Nara-e-Haideri! Ya Ali! Nara-e-Takbeer!*

The Japanese melted away under the impact of fire and steel. By dusk, the crest was back in Indian hands. Over the next 36 hours, sniping and mortar exchanges continued, but the position held.

Kagir Khan's war cry is an ancient Shiite rallying call to inspire courage and devotion. It means *Raise the slogan of Haider! Proclaim the slogan of God's greatness!* Haider is a name for Caliph Imam Ali, the son-in-law of the Prophet who was assassinated and is revered by Shias as the first Imam. For the men, however, the words needed no translation.

When the firing eased and the war cries from multiple faiths subsided, quieter work began. After every charge and attack, whether successful or not, came the men who kept the road open, the airstrips dry, and the wounded moving. Men like the Pioneers and the Madrasis in this war remain faceless to most accounts of the war because logistics and infrastructure are usually considered unglamorous. But their heroics were no less than those of the famed Pathan warriors.

Logistics: The Unglamorous Foundation for Victory

The Indian Pioneers worked where wheels stopped. In 4 feet of mud, at 5,000 feet of altitude, they carried rations, mortars, radios, wounded men. They laid tar, built airstrips, dug bunkers, and reinforced roadbeds. They moved without rest. Once, after returning from a full shift, 73 men were recalled within hours to unload a late convoy. They worked past midnight. Another time, rain turned the paddy into a lake, and petrol drums had to be rolled 800 yards through waist-deep floodwater. Former London University student Captain Donald Bishop, Indian Pioneer Corps, of 87, Mantilla Rd, Tooting London, SW 17, moved with the others, boots caught in the slush, hands to barrels. Five thousand gallons of gasoline reached the front that day.

Under fire, things got very tricky, and the Pioneers were adept at staying calm and getting the job done. At one drop zone near Imphal, shelling paused just long enough for nearly 100 Dakotas to unload their cargo. The Pioneers cleared the field before the guns resumed.

At Kohima, they delivered ammunition at night to infantry behind enemy lines, then returned the next evening to carry out the wounded. None were lost. In another action south of Silchar, a grenade burst beside a porter. The splinters pierced his water bottle but spared the man. It was amusing enough for the Pioneers to burst into laughter.

One Pioneer platoon spent 40 days collecting scattered supply drops across 3 square miles. In that time, they also carried the wounded over 100 miles of dense jungles and steep hills to the west of Ukhrul! Caught between friendly and enemy fire, they calmly retrieved most of the boxes of mis-dropped supplies. Another unit crossed a nullah under fire, delivering reserve rations on time. They evacuated over 100 casualties in a single night, over 3 miles through water and mud, stretchers on their heads. They arrived at the Regimental Aid Post greeting the Medical Officer with a smile and a song.

At Tamu, over 600 decomposing Japanese corpses lay in the open. The stench was unbearable, the sight uniformly ghastly. None of the Indian soldiers would approach, until the Chamar Pioneer Company, drawn from India's Dalit cobbler caste, stepped forward. With quicklime and fire, they cleared the site. They did it without complaint about the rampant caste prejudice and superstition.

Like the Pioneers, there were others too who kept the wheels turning: the drivers, mechanics, nurses, and clerks working quietly behind the scenes. Along every road and depot, I met Tamils like myself. The Madrasis were once renowned for their warrior traditions, at least upto the era of the Polygars and Pandyas in the 19th century. It was striking to see how vital they remained, even as non-combatants, to the battle to save India. The Madrasis were as different from the Sikhs as the latter were from the Gurkhas, and many of them weren't even fighting men. Yet they stood as living proof that India's strength lay in unity through diversity.

Wet to the bone, and quiet and self-effacing compared to the Punjabis and Rajputs, the Madrasis remained calm under fire. One offered me rice and sambhar from his pack, unasked. We spoke in Tamil for a few minutes. Then he returned to the mast he was repairing, as shells fell nearby.

The Madrasis are drivers and mechanics in the Royal Indian Army Service Corps, in the ordnance and supply depots, in the hospitals, in the Pioneers and in the Indian Air Force, not to mention the companies of the Madras Sappers and Miners and a battalion of the 3rd Madras Regiment which was defending Imphal to the north. New to modern warfare and yet with the earliest tradition in the Indian Army, these Madrasi infantrymen, besides killing a large number of Japanese, have patrolled far behind the enemy lines and brought back highly useful information.

Madrasis have distinguished themselves in the Indian Artillery too. Quite a large number of Madrasi officers were there serving in various arms if the army. Madrasi nurses did not lag behind their menfolk and they were there tending the sick and wounded with the care that is typical of them. Madras must be proud of these men and women they have sent in khaki and the part they have played in the winning of the battle of Manipur.

As an aside, one afternoon, when I was stationed elsewhere at the 14th Army HQ at Comilla in East Bengal, a group of West African troops sat cross-legged at dusk. They were from the same Royal West African Frontier Force that had helped defeat the Italians in Ethopia and Somaliland and then participated in our counter-offensive in Burma in 1943. As these tired warriors sat there, fresh from their exploits in the Kabaw Valley, Kali N. Ratnam's Tamil hit: *Ennadi Summa* (loosely translated as *Why are you dumb, my bonnie lassie?*) suddenly floated in the air.

Surprised at hearing a melody in my mother-tongue in a distant province, I made enquiries.

I found a stocky young Madrasi, Mr. J.D. Martin from Madurai who was running this YMCA center for the Africans, assisted by Mr. D.S. Vedanayagam, also from Madurai.

The Africans like Indian music with a quick tempo and they are interested in Indian life and history. Besides music parties, Mr. Martin arranges lectures and discussions for their benefit. In addition to a radio and a library, the Africans had plenty of recreation in the form of outdoor and indoor games.

Not many miles away was a similar YMCA center for Indian troops which was also run by another Madrasi, Mr. G. Eddy from Nagercoil. A feature of this center is its international dinner every fortnight when charming Indian nurses serve at dinner.

It was all very well to socialize to let off steam, but there were those of us fighting too far away to be invited to the party. And one could not forget others who were caught up in battle with no dog in the fight. We also came across thousands of unarmed refugees fleeing Japanese-occupied Burma, ragged dusty lines of men, women, and children with a few threadbare possessions and animals among them. They had endured trials of fire, starvation, and loss of family to finally reach what they thought was safety. They were innocents, bearing burdens as great as any soldier's, but without the means to fight back.

Refugees Attacked by All Sides

Poignant sagas of the war in South-East Asia are the stories of the flight of refugees from Japanese-occupied Burma. Escaping *from the Bushido* and his fire and facing our own fire, their one anxiety is to come over to our lines. With many an unknown hero or heroine among them, their deeds are equally heroic as that of any frontline soldier. Unarmed, shelled, machine-gunned and bombed, leaving behind their mothers, fathers, sisters, brothers and friends who are falling dead or wounded next to them, their one determination has been to reach our lines alive or dead. Aged, infirm, pregnant mothers, little children—all joined in this flight from the oppressor. With their indomitable courage nothing except death could stop them from reaching our lines.*

Typical of them is the story related to me by a charming 20-year-old girl from Burma. Her escape from the Japanese under the most trying circumstances is one of high courage and great determination but she has to remain unknown during the war. With her four younger sisters she left the Japanese lines at Myitkyina at midday telling the sentries that they were going to gather vegetables in the sacks they were carrying. Once the Japanese saw they were

---

*Bushido is the Japanese samurai's Way of the Warrior, a code of ethics emphasizing loyalty, courage and honor. In the Second World War, this manifested itself in extreme nationalism, refusal to give up, and a willingness to sacrifice one's life for the emperor, including kamikaze attacks.

escaping, they took pot-shots at them followed by volleys of machine-gunning them. Crawling on the ground to evade the bullets, the refugees had advanced a little when the shells from our lines came bursting on them. Once more lying flat during a lull they reached within a few yards of the Chinese lines who in turn started shooting at them. Crouching near a wall, these remarkable sisters quickly decided that the only expedient was to pinch the baby they were carrying. The baby cried and the Chinese stopped shooting. They were taken care of and fed by the Chinese till they were flown to India.

After witnessing the courage of those fleeing death, the final operations of the campaign unfolded. Roads and ridges were cleared and the Japanese forces were trapped as the 33 Corps pushed forward, in a series of advances built on both soldiers' heroism and the endurance of those caught in the crossfire.

By August, the tide that began at Imphal was flowing back toward victory.

Final Advances

Troops of the 33 Corps under Lieutenant General Montagu Stopford have cleared one more road of the Japanese: the 44 miles long road from Imphal to Ukhrul in the northwest.

While the Kohima-Imphal Road was the supply road from the rest of India to Manipur, the Ukhrul Road is one of the exits for the Japanese from the frontiers of India. The Devons flanking to the west of the road and proceeding north have contacted the King's Own Scottish Borderers (KOSBIs) who were coming south at Lamu, the 33 milestone on the road from Imphal. Ukhrul and the surrounding important features are now in our hands. After a tough battle on the August 8th, the 12th Frontier Force Regiment have occupied Chepu in which nearly 84 Japanese were killed and a number of POWs were captured.

*A battalion of 11th Sikh Regiment who have been honored recently for their activities in Burma with a Victoria Cross in the person of Naik Nand Singh. After a vigorous march along the hills to the west of the Ukhrul Road during which they killed many hundreds of Japanese, they have occupied Shangshak on the east side of the road. They cut across the road a few miles south of Ukhrul and proceeding via Lungshong reached Shangshak today. For quite a long time they have been supplied by air. Nearly as many as 300 Japanese have now been trapped to the west of the road.**

---

*Naik Nand Singh went on to participate in the Jammu and Kashmir operations in the 1947 Indo-Pak War, where on December 12, he led his platoon in a successful attack to

Naik Nand Singh

Indian and British troops of the 5th Indian Division have now cleared the 130-mile-long Silchar Track from Imphal to

---

extricate his battalion from an ambush. He was mortally injured by a close-quarters machine-gun burst, and posthumously awarded the Maha Vir Chakra. He was still wearing his Victoria Cross ribbon when his body was then paraded through the city of Muzaffarabad with a loudspeaker proclaiming that this would be the fate of every Indian VC. His corpse, thrown in a rubbish heap, was never recovered.

Silchar. The track is now clear of the Japanese on either side. Rajputs who fought well at Kohima, Punjabis and Dogras fresh from their battles near the south end of the Imphal-Kohima Road, fighting alongside equally famous British troops have cleared the track in less than three weeks. The Royal Engineers are sweeping the track for mines and the track is being attended to make it suitable for use in the monsoon.

To the Manipuri the track means much as it will bring him plenty of his betel-nuts, provisions, and fruits for winter. Once more coolies will run in relays of 16 miles on it carrying food in baskets swung on their backs. Originally only a bridal path the Army Engineers have made it a passable track and probably in the future a pukka metal road. Besides other things the Army has definitely improved the road communications from these plains surrounded by high hills and dense forests.

Of late it has been noticed that the Japanese have walked out of important positions without offering even a shadow of resistance in spite of the Orders of the Day of their commanders bidding them to capture Imphal. The famished, starved and stricken Japanese soldier knows that his hopes will prove futile. There are also indications from intelligence reports that his mind is afflicted by the doubt that he will never be able to recross the Chindwin to reach his dear ones at home.

I too have wondered when I will see my family again.

War is a test of endurance. What begins with bold attacks and ambitious plans sooner or later narrows to hunger, weariness, and the will to hold on. The Japanese soldier, once confident of reaching Imphal, now struggles to stay alive. Our men, hardened by months of siege and rain, continue their duty with a steadiness far beyond orders. It harks back to duty and honor, the virtues enshrined in our Gita.

The hills that once echoed with gunfire became quieter now. Villages began to stir again as the long lines of transport moved slowly along the repaired roads. As the enemy withdrew, they left behind their dead and their faith in victory. But our troops prevailed, tired, changed, and confident that this sacred ground had been held and would not be lost again. The triumph at Imphal was no occasion for pause, however, as we had to gather our wits and immediately mop up what was left.

Final Defeat of the Invaders[2]

Along the Tamu Road, the Japanese left under mist and rain. Burma's Kabaw Valley, already known to our men as the killing ground, lay ahead. The slopes down were muddy, and collapsed without warning. Exhausted and knee-deep in slush, some soldiers could not lie down without risking being swept away in the mud.

Split rice bags lay scattered beside the road. From some, paddy had begun to sprout. A Sikh jawan laughed. "Poor rats," he said, "no time to reap their harvest."

Ammunition crates, burned-out staff cars, pack saddles were strewn along the road. Some men picked through the wreckage for souvenirs, but most passed by ignoring the scene as if there was nothing new to see.

Pressing forward, the Patialas reached Ralph Hill. The wireless had failed, so the company commander sounded the bugle; the Japanese realized the attack only when our troops were within 250 yards. When it ended, 83 Japanese lay dead and 4 prisoners were taken beside lots of guns, wireless equipment, maps, and documents. A general's ribbon of the *Order of the Rising Sun* was found in an abandoned pack.

Along the Manipur Road, as Japanese forces fell back, Sikh, Jat, Dogra and Punjabi regiments advanced. Within 10 days, civilians began to receive salt, soap, cigarettes. Prices fell. At one point, a packet of cigarettes had cost two rupees. Now it cost six annas.

As the road was being opened by our troops, the Maharajah of Manipur led his temple gods in a procession with chanting and the sound of castanets and cymbals.

The enemy retreat turned to rout. In their retreat, the Japanese left behind guns, rations, tanks, wireless sets, and their dead scattered across the battlefields.

It is hard to understate the completeness with which the Japanese was beaten. He was in most cases starving and everywhere short of food. We came across a Japanese soldier barely clinging to life, paralyzed by beriberi, the result of surviving too long on nothing but polished rice.

In one encounter south of the Silchar track, a Japanese soldier lacking ammunition hurled stones at the advancing Punjabis. The soldier had to run to save his skin, and we Indians looked on with satisfaction.

The Japanese could not even take his guns with him, so great was his hurry. He abandoned some of his tanks. He discarded his wireless equipment and telephones. And his dead were scattered all over the battle areas.

On the other hand the morale of our troops is very high. After doubts due to the defeat in Burma and the lack of experience of newer recruits, the Indian soldier now knows he can fight under the most rigorous conditions. "Our men remain in excellent fighting spirit and the enemy is no match for them," a Viceroy Commissioned Officer from Kohat in the Northwest Frontier Province told me.

In ambushes, our men proved cleverer; in reconnaissance, they returned valuable intelligence unseen. In raids, small groups inflicted heavy casualties on superior forces, and in frontal attacks, companies swept to victory with bayonets. Even in the element of surprise the enemy has been outwitted.

On the road back from Manipur, children stood beside the culverts. Some clapped. One held a flag on a bamboo stick. The soldiers passed without words. I gave the children a few boiled sweets. Some of the older ones would have preferred cigarettes.

The old "frontier" lay west, across the Khyber. Now another had emerged, with steep ridges and wet jungle, east of Assam. Few had imagined fighting here, and even fewer expected to return. My report was necessarily triumphalist in tone, but I felt it was justified.

Unfortunately, owing to the attention of the world being focused on events elsewhere, the importance and true magnitude of the Battle of Manipur has not been appreciated. On a front extending to nearly 300 miles three Japanese divisions have been beaten and thrown out, the Japanese suffering nearly 50,000 casualties. General Slim's 14th Army troops, British and Indian, who fought there know how they had to fight both a maleficent monsoon as well as a powerful foe. When the lotus blooms in the ponds of Manipur and the coy maidens along the roads smile as they throw their fishing nets into the lakes from where the enemy is now far removed, our troops understand it to be an expression of their gratitude.

Gratitude, more than popularity, has moved the men. Their joy, however, is tempered by exhaustion and the knowledge that every gain has been hard-won. Though the war will undoubtedly end, what comes after could be anyone's guess.

To understand the Indian soldier one has to know his military tradition both in the Indian Army and in Indian history. He is proud of his noble past and heritage. Coupled with his high sense of duty and his philosophy of life, this is what makes him valiant and has contributed to his success in Eritrea, El Alamein, Benghazi, Tobruk, Italy and Manipur. Destiny rules him and to die as a warrior is his greatest honor. And yet no hallowed past, no story of destiny, is enough to justify his final breath.

5

Kyaukse–Meiktila Sector[1]

March–May 1945

Armoured and infantry columns push through the Kyaukse plain and the central Dry Zone, isolating Japanese forces and forcing their retreat toward the Irrawaddy and Rangoon axis.

The defense of India was over. The tide that had broken against the hills of Manipur now began to flow east.

In 1942, the refugees fled along the roads on which we were now marching. Many of them were Indians, including women who were raped by the Burmese, and some, especially children, had perished along the way, felled by gunfire, disease, and starvation. That same year, the British, supported by Chinese troops, were forced to retreat nearly 900 miles across Burma, finally crossing back to India. General Slim was head of the Burma Corps then, and he had to learn a bitter lesson from that defeat. Along the way, they lost most of their equipment and transport. The only positive from the Allied standpoint was that they managed to burn not only Burma's treasured oil-fields, but anything else including granaries and food stocks the Japanese could get their hands on. The Burmese were left impoverished, victims of a war that was not of their making.

The Burmese people would pay another terrible price under the Japanese for their misplaced loyalty. Meanwhile, a dark period of Allied defeat and failed counter-attack would last three years. In September 1942, General Archibald Wavell, Commander-in-Chief in India, ordered the Eastern Army in India to attack Burma's Arakan in Rakhine State and to capture enemy airfields on Akyab Island in Sittwe. The first goal was achieved, but the British were then hit by a valiant Japanese counter-attack and they had to withdraw back to India by March 1943.

The hard lessons of the Arakan failure, however, spawned new, unconventional ideas. Deep behind the lines, a different kind of war was being waged. In 1943-44, Major General Orde Wingate's Chindits had been carrying out daring guerilla tactics behind enemy lines in Burma. Their successes came with very high Chindit casualties, but their presence in Burma rattled the Japanese.

Two years of relentless fighting later, the great tide of the war had finally turned. The years between retreat and return had hardened both our armies and our resolve. And now, in March 1945, I was in Central Burma. It was a place of great beauty, and I was struck by the serenity of Buddhist temples, where some refugees had taken shelter. I also saw striking, sarong-clad women wearing a beguiling *thanaka* paste on their faces. But nothing, not even Buddhist forbearance, could hide their pain, for they had felt the full brunt of Japanese atrocities.

Fortunately for the Burmese, this time it was the Japanese who, having been defeated in India, were retreating across Burma. As for us, the morale of our troops was understandably high. Like the ancient Aryans of the Rig-Veda who used fire to conquer the Gangetic lands, praising its excellent and refulgent purity, it was we who now worshipped the splendor of (gun) fire.

We were back on the same roads that had once carried our soldiers' humiliating retreat, only now we were travelling in the opposite direction. The hills and chaungs that were silent witnesses to our flights and failed counter-attacks now watched us advance. And the Burmese who

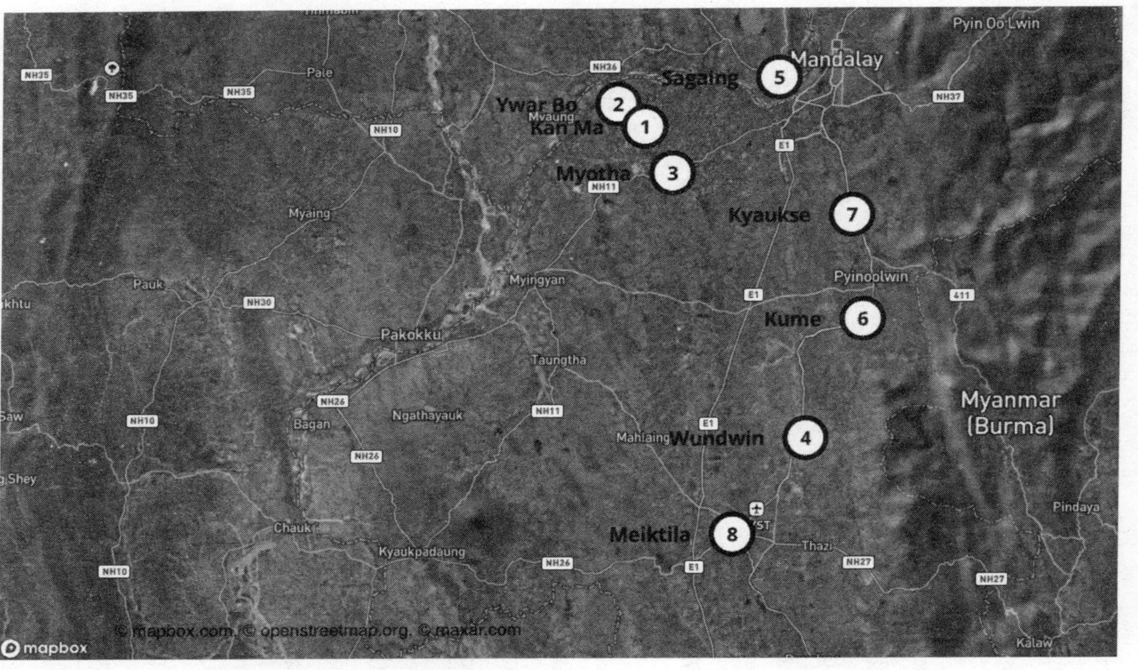

Battle narrative map: Mandalay to Meiktila

had once turned against Indians were waiting by the roadside, offering what little food they had, whispering where the Japanese had passed.

Among the Indians who advanced together were gunners and sepoys, Gurkha warriors and sappers, doctors and nurses. It was like a large family, at times even a highly skilled circus, travelling colorfully and valiantly through this battered land.

Encircled and Erased, March 7

An outstanding joint operation by Gurkhas of the 1st Gurkha Rifles and British tanks from the Royal Armored Corps succeeded in capturing a well-defended Japanese position west of Sinbyugon. As one troop of tanks and a company of Gurkhas cut off the Japanese retreat, the rest of the infantry advanced on the other flank led by another squadron of tanks. The enemy bolted into tall grass, where they became invisible. The Gurkhas closed in, kukris drawn, shouting their terrifying battle cry *Jai Mahakali, Ayo Gorkhali* (*Victory to Goddess Mahakali, the Gurkhas are Upon You!*). As with a sickle they literally reaped the harvest. The enemy used LMG fire and sniped without much effect. Seventy-two Japanese were killed, while only two were taken alive, but wounded. Two anti-tank guns were captured.

This operation, made possible by accurate reconnaissance from Gurkha and Frontier scouts, underscored the precision and coordination behind the Indian Army's advance across central Burma. As we advanced, the landscape itself seemed haunted by the remnants of the retreating enemy, the silent villages and abandoned fields of Burma witnessing the tragic doings of men.

In a coordinated advance toward Kan Ma (@1 in *Battle Narrative Map: Mandalay to Meiktila*)*, 45 miles west of Mandalay, British troops captured three additional villages. Resistance was light, but the operation moved methodically. I observed the engagement for Anaktau from a forward position.*

The infantry advanced under covering fire from Jat units positioned on the right flank. Our tanks provided support. As the approach began, the Japanese opened fire with small arms. Our response came through mortar rounds and machine gun bursts. An interlude amid the din of battle was marked by the neighing of a solitary mule.

During the initial push, a wounded Japanese soldier was evacuated in one of our jeep ambulances. A second was taken prisoner later. Nearly 100 Japanese troops attempted to escape across the creek or chaung east of Anaktau. As they stepped into the water, our artillery engaged. Results of this pounding have not yet come in.

Each new encounter exposed the unraveling discipline of the once-formidable Japanese forces. Near Ywar Bo (@2 in *Battle Narrative Map: Mandalay to Meiktila*), one of their final attempts at organized defense faltered under steady machine-gun fire.

The war that had once been fought inch by inch was now a moving hunt. Each day's march erased the map of occupation a little further. Yet as we advanced, we had no idea how much longer the battle would continue.

The Beginning of the End, March 10

By the time we reached Ywar Bo, the pursuit was no longer war as we had known it. We were witnessing the complete unraveling of a once-glorious army. We observed three tell-tale signs of a force facing defeat:

The Japanese had been disarming the wounded and weak among their comrades and leaving them behind, either to fend for themselves or to throw themselves at the mercy of one of our ambulances.

A recently captured Japanese soldier revealed that two days in Japan and three months in Singapore was the only training he had been given.

They also did not seem to have received their mail for quite a long time. The latest date one interrogating officer noticed among their letters was "Japan, October 1944."

No amount of training can withstand the soul-crushing burden of defeat. We were now witnessing the beginning of the end of the Japanese Imperial Army in Burma.

A Japanese convoy attempting to entrench itself last night on the perimeter outside Ywar Bo came under heavy machine gun fire from Indian troops. Leading the charge was Subedar Abdul Razaak, elder brother of the late Jemadar Abdul Hafiz, Victoria Cross, of the 9th Jat Regiment. Both men were Muslim Rajputs from Rohtak District, Punjab.

Razaak's platoon, part of a machine gun section, opened fire as the enemy began digging in. Havildar Mubarak Ali also of Rohtak, was among the gunners. Five Japanese were confirmed killed; others were wounded and fled into the darkness.

Ahead lay the Irrawaddy River, broad, brown, and swollen with the season's rains. Every campaign in Burma led, sooner or later, to a river, and each river crossing tested our resolve.

The Crossing Under Fire, March 10–16

Major M. Hiauddin of the 12th Frontier Force Regiment, of Peshawar, led a complex but swift night operation resulting in the capture of Yezin and Inya villages. His unit encountered a fortified enemy position guarding the only crossing over a chaung leading to Yezin. The approach was mined, and our sappers had to first clear it. Infantry then had to secure the position before the engineers could prepare the crossing for tanks. These operations had to be carried out at great speed due to enemy shelling. The battle lasted 12 hours.

Once the crossing was taken, the battalion rapidly consolidated gains and altered its axis of advance to target Inya, southwest of Yezin. Despite heavy enemy shelling over a 12-hour battle window, Major Hiauddin remained cool and composed under fire. They killed nearly 150 Japanese and captured a 105 mm gun.

Having secured the crossings, our forces pressed into the heart of central Burma, which became the stage for sporadic clashes as retreating Japanese forces were systematically routed.

The crossings, however, were only the start of the challenge: the terrain and climate remained a persistent enemy.

Our troops are fighting in rocky undulating country interspersed with mango orchards with the smell of fresh blossoms, banana groves and ripe tomato gardens. Palm trees are the only heights and the ground is mostly shrubbery. As we advance, the Burmese are returning to their villages that we have recovered from the enemy.

Very small one-foot diameter wells abound but the water is not potable. Drinking water is therefore efficiently rationed.

Elsewhere, an armored reconnaissance patrol led by Captain Mohammad Ashraf Jan of Peshawar, a veteran of the Western Desert and former POW of the Nazi Panzers in Libya, covered 14 miles. At each village, the locals showed him the enemy positions. In one, the villagers waving their dahs (long knives), shouted and pointed out the enemy who were bolting on the road with their 70 mm gun loaded on a bullock-cart that they had confiscated! As the enemy took to their heels, Captain Ashraf Jan's guns plastered them, killing three Japanese and wounding many more. Our men captured the gun and an officer's writing-case that had plenty of pictures in it. The villagers returned with the cart and bullocks. They were very hospitable and offered Captain Jan and his team nearly 20 eggs, refusing to accept any price for them.

At the monastery town of Myotha (@3), an armored raiding column of the 20th Indian Division got to work. The column was composed of troops of the 10th Gurkha Rifles as well as the 18th King Edward VII's Own Cavalry, which had played a distinguished role in 1942 as part of the 3rd Indian Motor Brigade at Bir Hakim in the Libyan desert. I joined the column near a patch in the wilderness about 2 miles north of Myotha where they were poised to strike.

It was a moonless cold night and as I lay on a truck, I saw the sky above dancing with shooting stars while on the skyline, huge fires were raging on three sides of us. My ears were subjected to a symphony consisting of the din of our own guns and the muffled peals of an airstrike that our bombers were making a few miles away. In between, this weird music of war there was an eerie quiet disturbing to the mind. I was reminded of civilization only by the "rat-a-tat" of a bullock-cart as a Burmese villager drove along the road shouting "hey hey." Perhaps he was coming away from his village with all his belongings since the enemy had set fire to it. Of late, the enemy has been attempting to scorch as many villages as possible in the wake of his retreat.

Last night our patrols reported that there was no sign of the enemy in the north-east monastery area of the town. This morning I set out with the column, not in the armored cars which were making their way across fields, gardens and chaungs, but in a Dodge truck that accompanied them. In less than an hour, we reached the center of town after taking a devious route in order to avoid enemy observation. We passed a pagoda and several buildings razed to the ground as a result of Japanese vandalism. I noticed the precalculated effects of our bombing too and it was quite easy to discern the chivalrous hand of the Bushido!

Utter desolation hung over the town as we drove down the road with not even a crow to run away frightened at our arrival. Life seemed to be dead in our vicinity till the cheerful Sikh driver next to me cut a joke with his friend behind.

We now occupy what was previously a Burmese cotton mill which has been reduced to ashes. About 20 yards away, a smoldering fire marks the last remains of a bale of cotton.

This was once a place of industry, and now it had been needlessly destroyed.

In the southeast near Natthdaw (March 16), a forward formation under Major-General Gracey's 20th Indian Division pushed 7 miles east of the Sagaing–Myotha railway. The force captured nine guns, including howitzers, anti-tank weapons, and battalion artillery. Alongside these were 17 lorries, one staff car, personal belongings of a senior Japanese officer, and a cache of documents. Infantry, tanks, and artillery inflicted heavy but hard-to-quantify casualties. A big battle continued east of Natthdaw into the evening.

General Gracey, a man who was usually accompanied by his friendly black Labrador, praised the performance of his troops, remarking on their speed and complexity of maneuver. The operations, he said, had routed many Jap gun crews besides killing a large number. of the enemy. Raised especially to fight in Burma, these troops were renowned Japanese killers and they remained proud of their record. A significant factor to notice were the increasing number of prisoners being captured.

The pressure on retreating forces was mounting. With each road cut, each gun captured, and each position secured, the noose tightened around the remnants of the Japanese Army in Burma. Roads once defended by disciplined detachments now lay open, with abandoned rifles, carts, and scattered supplies marking the speed of their retreat. In addition to guns and abandoned supplies, empty homes and buildings bore witness to lives abruptly halted.

The Irrawaddy crossing had cost us men and craft, but the line held. Once that was over, we regrouped in the flat central basin west of Wundwin, where the next Japanese rearguard was already digging in.

The March for Wundwin, March 21

The 20th Indian Division advanced from Chaungwwa toward Wundwin (@4). Indian armored cars, British and Indian tanks, Royal Artillery, and infantry from the 10th Gurkha Rifles and Bombay Grenadiers formed the column. I accompanied this column on their nearly 60 mile march from Chaungwwa and all along we met with very little opposition—though a few stragglers fired at us before they could be either dispersed or killed.

Near Pinze, our advance guard contacted odd parties of Japanese infiltrating east. Several were killed, and two prisoners we took later died of their injuries. The first night, our tanks and Gurkhas laid a road-block 3 miles east of Pinze on the main road. Two ammunition-carrying Japanese trucks were blown up and two captured in running order. Twenty bullock-carts carrying equipment were also destroyed. Soon after, we reached Wundwin.

Occupying Wundwin today, an armored column of the 20th Indian Division has driven a wedge between Japanese forces operating in the Kyaukse and Meiktila areas. Opposition was slight—a party of 30 Japanese who were completely surprised and found digging in. The enemy started running, but five of them were killed before the village was cleared. Truckloads of enemy ordnance stores and medical equipment have been found. The booty includes a number of vehicles in good running order, including some we left behind in 1942, as well as valuable engineering equipment.

A village headman reported that the fleeing Japanese told him a vast American army was at their heels, which was the reason for their panic.

It must be remembered that Wundwin lies on one of the exit routes for the Japanese towards the Shan States, whose heights I could see from here against the skyline.

At Pindale, 22 miles west of Wundwin, the Bombay Grenadiers engaged Japanese remnants and had a good kill. They captured seven swords and likely accounted for more lives than that number. In this attack, Naik Ramji Lal, a Jat of Laudhari, Isar district, came upon three Japanese officers armed only with swords and shot at them. A medical and ordnance dump was seized, and our troops went in to fetch their correct size of boots.

Some soldiers who seemed to disappoint turned out to be surprisingly effective. Jemadar Jayakishen, a Jat from Khairampur, Isar district, when chided by his company commander for firing nearly 300 rounds without producing a dead Japanese, went back, chased a few, and returned dragging two enemy dead.

The march of the column has so completely surprised the enemy that he has not been given enough time to range his guns against us as we have not heard his artillery since we left Chaungwwa.

Battling on the Riverbank, March 25

Holding a flank as two divisions of the 14th Army crossed the Irrawaddy River further south, a battalion of the 3rd Madras Regiment fought against elaborate defenses that the Japanese had established on the riverbank near

Sagaing (@5). Enemy defenses included anti-tank ditches, long connecting tunnels with machine-gun posts, and numerous devilish 250- and 500-pound aerial bombs set with trip-wires. The whole area was heavily mined. Supported by tanks of the Royal Armored Corps, the Madrasis had to attack a village, Pegado, in this area.

They first cleared a cactus-covered position on the left before launching the main attack. With air cover and 37 mm howitzers, and the Madras Sappers and Miners clearing the mines, they advanced. Very soon the entire village was blazing under our fire.

Sepoy Nookanna of Visakhapatnam, with the forward platoon, noticed three Japanese in one bunker. He crept to the nearest tank and tapped on the turret. A British gunner cautiously craned his neck out and asked, "Hello Johnny, what is it?" Nookanna pointed at the bunker, and the tank immediately gave a burst, killing all three. The rest of the Japanese, about 50, fled in panic.

When our troops entered the village after the fires died down, they found nearly 200 bunkers. This attack culminated in their eventual arrival at Sagaing.

Further south along the Irrawaddy at Kanlan Ywathit, we saw even more action.

Soon after we crossed the Irrawaddy, the Japanese initiated a series of savage assaults supported by artillery, medium guns, and flame throwers. A battalion of the 13th Frontier Force Rifles beat them back over 48 hours of fierce combat, finally wresting our position.

A platoon of the 17th Dogras nipped in the bud a Japanese force calling themselves *Teishintai*,* with motives of long-range penetration behind our lines. About 40 of them were caught bathing in a river by the Dogras. They charged and killed many of the enemy who started running in panic. A little later, the Dogras laid an ambush and killed more of this force.

At Letkapin, a company of the 10th Gurkha Rifles witnessed a grim spectacle. After a stiff fight that killed over 90 Japanese, 35 of the enemy, rather than surrender, walked into the river and drowned themselves with their kits on. The Gurkhas looked on amusedly and fired a few rounds to make sure the drowning men did not rise again! Elsewhere, Gurkhas of the 8th Rifles charged three enemy 150-mm guns while they were firing and killed the entire gun crew. The guns lay silent with the beheaded bodies of their comrades**.

---

*Japanese special forces, part of the Imperial Japanese Army Air Force. Most were parachuted in to carry out ground operations.
**While probably not war crimes on the part of the Gurkhas, the events at Letkapin do illustrate the savagery on both sides.

Indian and British cavalry, dashing across country, continually harried the retreating enemy, killing hundreds and capturing guns and stores. Once, when an Indian tank knocked against an enemy machine-gun bunker, the crew climbed down, killed the Japanese inside, and then resumed their post, bringing the gun with them.

Every arm and every service contributed its share to the success of the Division. Indian Signals laid cables under the Irrawaddy, sinking them every 10 yards with improvised weights, all under shellfire and strafing. Artillery units often fought like infantry; one mountain-gun detachment surprised 10 Japanese at their meal, killing four with tommy guns and grenades. Doctors, nurses, and medical orderlies worked tirelessly, often giving their own blood for the wounded. Motor-transport and supply personnel cooperated efficiently to ensure the success of the Division's drive.

When the last enemy positions along the bank were cleared, our troops moved through the abandoned bivouacs and supply dumps. The scale of material left behind told its own story.

Abandoned Camps, March 25

Killing nearly 400 Japanese and capturing 23 prisoners, an armored column of the 20th Indian Division captured Kume (@6), 19 miles south of Kyaukse. A large enemy headquarters had been taken by surprise, so much so that a half-eaten meal was discovered in a Japanese officer's mess. The booty included 5 staff-cars, 18 motor transports, 25 outboard motors, and 16 assault boats. As we celebrated the haul, the rest of the enemy at Kume fled eastwards. Our troops also found two abandoned trains complete with engines and coal containing wagonloads of ammunition. Most shameful of all was their hurried evacuation of a hospital, leaving behind 23 of their wounded men.

Amid the wreckage, life carried on with grim absurdity. Soldiers found sweetness in abandoned bakeries, and death in a cup of toddy.

Jam Puffs and Poisoned Toddy (March 29, 1945)

Three British cooks and a Color Sergeant took up their rifles and walked off with a forward platoon to beat off a fierce Japanese attack. They were: Private Ronald Salvidge of 35 Cotton Mill Crescent, St. Albans, Herts; Lance Corporal Robert Stevenson of 26 Kelvinside Crescent,

Banton, Kilsyth, Stirlingshire; Private Tom Stanley of 1 Chain Bar Road, Hattersley, Hyde, Cheshire; and Colour Sergeant Raymond Henley of 2 Rynsford Road, Dallington, Northampton.

On the Irrawaddy bridgehead, about 40 Japanese lined up in the night and started digging in some 100 yards outside our perimeter when our machine guns opened fire. Thereafter, the Japanese launched three fierce attacks—screaming and yelling, supported by grenades and medium machine guns—but they were beaten back.

Next morning, we counted 14 dead Japanese. "Killing Japs was certainly a good change over from the frying pan," one of the cooks told me while handing me a hot jam puff.

A retreat of an occupying army revives its people. The Burmese, who had so often turned on Indians living among them, now gaunt and starved and tired of suffering, welcomed us with open arms. Meanwhile, they provided vital intelligence, ratted on the Japanese, and helped kill them off with small acts of sabotage. I saw a report that villagers of a certain area poisoned nearly 50 Japanese with medicated toddy that first stupefies and then kills the victim.

Meanwhile, south of Mandalay, our columns struck at Kyaukse, with its railway junction and supply dumps, forcing the Japanese to abandon their hold on the approach to Mandalay.

Battle for Kyaukse, March 25–29

Kyaukse (@7) lies 31 miles south of Mandalay on the trunk road to Rangoon. The railway also runs through the town. Its population in 1930 was nearly 7,500. Its importance to the retreating Japanese is also that it serves as the exit gateway for their disorganized troops from central Burma into the hills of the Shan States.

While the Japanese are generally disorganized elsewhere, those further north at Kyaukse are offering stiff resistance. It is apparently a major enemy base with numerous ammunition, supply, and ordnance dumps. The Japanese are trying to evacuate as much as possible and probably have been ordered to hold the rest to the last.

A vast area to the west of the town, between the railway and the Panlaung River, appears to be one enormous ammunition dump. Ammunition in large quantities has been stored by the enemy in villages surrounding Kyaukse, under bushes, beside roads and trees, under any cover available, dispersed in small stocks. Many of these have been destroyed by our troops, some captured intact, and the rest are still in enemy hands, accounting for his grim resistance.

It is a curious picture on this front: at one place the Japanese are running away, pursued by our armored column; in another, they are holding on with great strength. Kyaukse is being heavily shelled by us and bombed from the air. The enemy too is shelling our forward troops.

Last week, troops from the Northwest Frontier supported by British tanks cleared an area near Kyaukse in the face of considerable opposition from snipers and slew nearly 50 Japanese.

In spite of stubborn Japanese resistance, 14th Army troops gradually closed in on Kyaukse from the north, west, and south. On March 28, against considerable opposition, Gurkhas captured Kade, a village 3 miles to the southwest of the town. They captured a light machine gun and counted five dead Japanese.

Unfortunately, the battle was never going to be easy. The whole of Kyaukse district is covered by a network of irrigation canals originally constructed by the Burmese as early as 1000 AD. Most of these channels have been remodeled on modern lines. The river Zawgyi flows through the town itself, and the large number of sluices have enabled the enemy to inundate particular areas, making it difficult for our tanks to operate. Yet our soldiers fought against all odds.

Two Dogra Rajputs—Havildar Mangal Singh of village Pindi Deonia, District Sialkot, and Lance Naik Vir Singh of village Dugan, District Kathua, Jammu State—received congratulations from General Slim, Commander of the 14th Army, for their gallantry. They were also awarded the Indian Distinguished Service Medal (IDSM) and the Military Medal (MM) respectively.

Havildar Mangal Singh, with six others, went to investigate a local report about Japanese activity. When they reached a nullah, his leading scouts reported the enemy sitting in it. He crawled forward, and noticing 50 to 60 Japanese, made a thorough reconnaissance of the area. Then, taking the initiative and keeping half a section behind to give him covering fire, he attacked with only four men, shouting in English: "One company to the right! One company to the left! Charge!" Believing nearly two companies were attacking them, the enemy withdrew 200 to 300 yards.

Meanwhile, the Havildar killed two and brought back their pistols. Since the enemy were too many for him, he withdrew about 100 yards and sent for company support. He kept up the fire and beat back one attack before the company turned up an hour later. They killed 22 Japanese, including an officer, and wounded another 10 before returning with a large booty of rifles and light machine guns.

Lance Naik Vir Singh was with the leading section in the company attack, and though severely wounded in the thigh, led his section in a charge and himself bayonetted two of the enemy.

Our Dogras reached the railway station and inventoried enemy stores in a register left behind. Gurkhas and Punjabis took the junction near Myauk Hamyinbo. They began converging from north and south, aiming to link up and clear the nearly 52 miles of road from Mandalay to Rangoon.

The last Japanese train did not leave Kyaukse station. It was loaded with 23 boxes of sewing machines, medical stores, electrical goods, clothing, photographic material, pictorial journals, large quantities of paper—enough to last an entire school for a year—and mess furniture, including sofa settees.

Some of its passengers lay with their bones scattered all over the station yard.

Kyaukse's fall opened the way to Meiktila, a name that, to me, will always mean both courage and ruin.

Heroism at Meiktila, April–May

The battle for Meiktila (@8) marked a decisive turn. In the annals of the Indian Army, Meiktila will always be remembered as the battlefield where the heroism and might of the Indian soldier were at its height. To both us and the enemy, the battle for Meiktila turned out to be the battle for Burma.

In this shattered city, Sepoy Fazl Din of the 10th Baluch Regiment was attacked by enemy fire from bunkers. He demolished one bunker with grenades and as he was attacking the others with his men, enemy soldiers sprang out from a house, with two of them brandishing swords. As one Japanese officer savaged the company commander with his sword, Fazl Din rushed to the rescue, engaging him in hand-to-hand combat. The Japanese officer ran Fazl Din through the chest with his sword, but the Naik still managed to kill the officer and two others and continued to direct his section's attack until he collapsed and died from his wounds.

His platoon, having witnessed one of the most remarkable acts of courage in war, surged forward and wiped out the Japanese garrison.

For this act, Fazl Din received the Victoria Cross posthumously. His battalion, almost half of which were Punjabi Muslims, accounted for, according to statistics I was shown, more than 500 Japanese dead in the Meiktila sector alone.

Naik Fazl Din is the third Muslim in this war to receive this highest award for gallantry. With this, Major General Cowan's Black Cats have won seven of them. In a special Order of the Day announcing the award, Major General Cowan declared: "On behalf of all ranks of the 17th Indian Division I warmly congratulate the 10th Baluch on this great distinction which their record as a fighting battalion in operations against the Japanese has fully merited. I voice the feelings of all ranks in saying how much I regret this gallant NCO did NOT live to enjoy the honor." Naik Fazl Din's widow, 22-year-old Sirdar Bibi, will be the proud though tragic recipient of the Victoria Cross so gallantly won by her late husband.

This 24-year-old, tall, well-built, light-skinned and cheerful son of a small farmer of Hussainpur (Hoshiarpur district, Punjab) showed early promise of a soldier even when he was working on his father's fields. He was about 18 when one night a party of 10 dacoits attacked his village. Chasing them, he broke the leg of one with a heavy stick and handed him over to the village policeman. Among his playmates and other boys of the village, he was always the leader and they implicitly carried out his orders. His favorite pastime was to accost the boys returning from the village school in the evenings, snatch their football from them and after kicking it for a short while, return it to them.

Naik Fazl Din lost his parents when he was a boy of eight. His ambition was to join the army and one cold day in 1940, he and a cousin stole out of the village without any counsel and enlisted at the nearest recruiting office. Though a volunteer, he had planned to remain in the army. Even while under training, he had been picked out of the rest by his Subedar and he won the first prize for high-jump in his batch of recruits. He has fought with his battalion in Burma in 1942, in the Chin Hills in 1943, in Imphal in 1944 and once again in Burma in 1945. While at Tiddim, he received the Commando Badge, the battalion's award for the best patrolling.

Major S.K. Korla, DSO, Military Cross (MC), of the 10th Baluch also distinguished himself here. A tall, smiling 27-year-old, he spoke freely of his battalion's exploits but needed coaxing to mention his own. Born into a Dogra military family, he was an outstanding cadet at the Indian Military Academy, praised for "the finest martial spirit." He won the DSO in 1942 for leading bayonet charges under fire and retrieving ammunition from enemy lines, later earning a mention in dispatches for escorting a mule convoy 57 miles under pursuit. In 1945, he received the MC for a surprise attack at Taungtha that captured enemy dumps with minimal losses.

Now, at Magygon, near Meiktila, he cleared a fortified village in 15 minutes under heavy fire. Later at Point 850 nearby, he charged through scrub jungle and across deep nullahs to silence a key Japanese observation post, killing 63 and capturing 2. His Dogra company killed 364 Japanese and took 23 prisoners.

Our Black Cats not only won 7 Victoria Crosses in Burma but earned 409 awards in toto by war's end. At Meiktila West, one company killed 138 Japanese in a single day. Their advance southward was relentless.

Amid acts of bravery, the grim cost of retreat was starkly visible along rivers and roads, where the dead lay rotting and uncared for, exposed to the elements and devoured by scavengers.

With Meiktila taken, the campaign's tempo shifted from advance to endurance. Oppressive heat, rot, and fever became as deadly as bullets. Rangoon lay ahead, its steaming and storied capital awaiting our arrival, at whatever cost.

6

Pegu–Rangoon Corridor*

April–August 1945

The fighting along the Pegu line systematically broke Japanese defenses, clearing the last obstacle before Rangoon.

The push to Rangoon began on April 9. At Shwemyo Bluff (Milestone 271), resistance was encountered. Instead of launching a frontal assault, the regiment bypassed the position via a 25-mile night march and rejoined the main road further south. Pyinmana followed. There, Indian armor targeted the Japanese 33rd Army HQ while

*Japanese special forces, part of the Imperial Japanese Army Air Force. Most were parachuted in to carry out ground operations

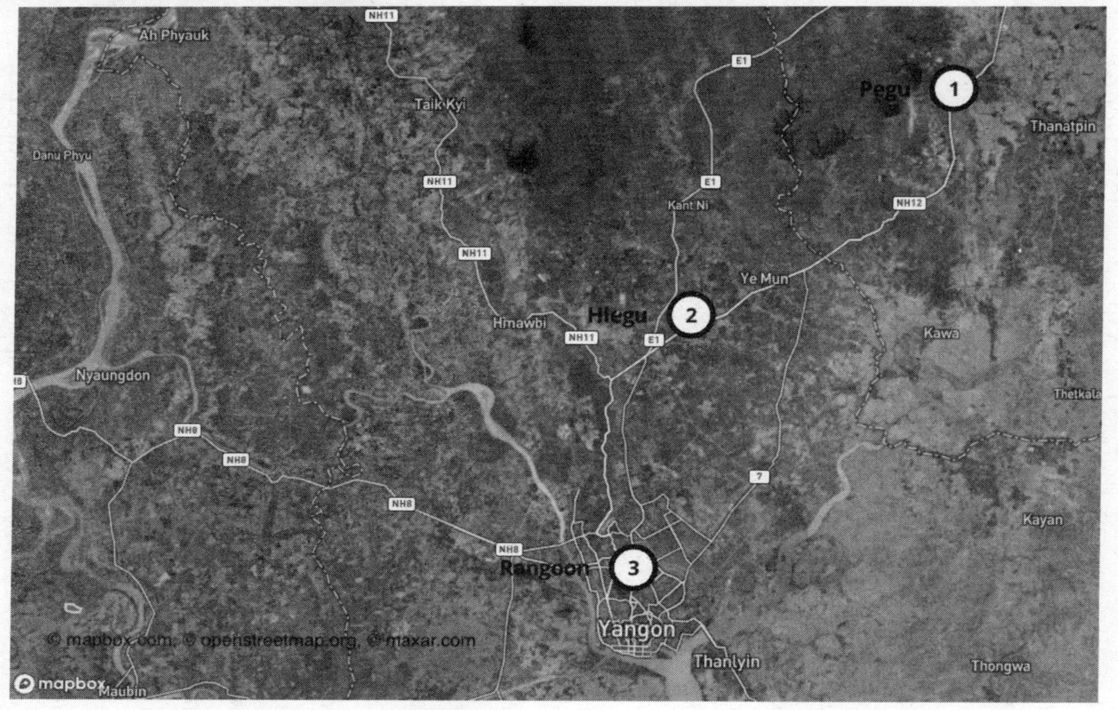

Battle narrative map: The Road to Rangoon

Punjabi troops cut the road at Milestone 227. Twelve Japanese were killed near the road-block; another 20 fell near the Lewe airstrip.

The Pegu (or Bago) Yomas hills are not more than 1,000 feet in height but rise into steep narrow ridges on which runs the only navigable track. The terrain is covered with thick scrub, dense bamboo jungles and tall elephant grass. Numerous chaungs crisscross the area, flowing in spate. Wild elephants roam here, destroying bamboo jungles and causing a heavy din which resounds in the quiet forest. The sight and sound will strike despair in a humiliated and frustrated spirit.

Starved, armed with too few rifles (as few as 40 shared among 70 men), and pursued from above and below, the remnants of the Japanese 15th Army roamed this harrowed landscape, harried by British shells and Burmese guerrillas. One Japanese soldier wrote:

"I am a warrior of the Imperial Army and I am not one to complain of any shortage of food but seeing my comrades complaining of shortage and losing their trust in their officers, it makes me think that this Burma campaign has done more to damage the spirit of the Imperial Army than anything else."

Villagers also ambushed patrols and removed wheels from enemy guns. The Karen hillmen watched silently from their bamboo huts, sometimes handing over captured Sten guns. Gurkhas gave close support to these insurgents.

Soldiers from each side appeared sometimes in mufti, but for different reasons. Further east, Sepoy Jumme Shah of Jhelum was taken captive while dressing the wounds of a comrade. He escaped his captors during a barrage, disguised himself in borrowed Burmese clothing, and limped back through a village of 400 Japanese to his unit. In another instance, a jeep driver from Bihar captured a disguised Japanese officer who dropped a grenade from his robe.

Near Pegu (or Bago) (@1 in *Battle Narrative Map: The Road to Rangoon)* of the 12th Frontier Force Regiment crossed the Pegu River under fire, using trollies and rafts after bridges were blown. They killed 89 Japanese in two days. Their improvised trolley supply line, dubbed the "Pegu Express," carried supplies and prisoners.

A Punjabi platoon under Subedar Mohd. Fazal of Montgomery district captured enemy bunkers on the Pegu River's banks and repelled several counterattacks.

It happened about 12 miles northwest of Pegu on the thickly jungled banks of the river bearing the same name. In their first clash with 25 Japanese, they killed 1 and wounded 2 more, before the enemy dispersed. While sections of the platoon were reconnoitering the area, another party of 50 Japanese attacked the main platoon from the rear with LMGs, rifles and grenade dischargers. The Subedar gradually withdrew his men to where he discovered a few vacant bunkers with Japanese kits still lying about. He decided to stay in them for the night. From this strong defensive position, the Subedar and his men held the enemy fire and beat off one attack when the enemy tried to rush the position. The enemy was forced to withdraw with heavy casualties.

"We got in before the Japanese did. They lost the position and so lost the battle," he told me.

In the chaos, some Japanese soldiers chose to drown rather than surrender. At Letkapin, 35 men walked in rows into a river and vanished beneath it. The Gurkhas fired a few rounds to ensure they would not rise again. *Tamam shudh.* There too, a Japanese gun crew had been beheaded beside their 150 mm weapon, the sword placed neatly between them. This was clearly the handiwork of Gurkhas.

Amid these horrors, life still went on in quieter corners, where noncombatants continued their essential work, reminding us that the campaign was sustained by many firm hands behind the battlefield. Among such decay, even the simplest gestures of care became key to restoring our faith.

The Barber and His Wars

He was known simply as Shah Mohamed, a barber of village Jindala, district Gujrat, a civilian, and part of the 5th Indian Division. Punjabi by birth, 50 years old, and entirely toothless, he carried no rank, no weapon. What he did carry, always, was a wooden box filled with clippers, scissors, combs, and the detritus of a profession honed across three continents of war.

He had been with the army since the early years of the campaign in Eritrea. From there, he followed the 4th Division into North Africa, cutting hair near Tobruk, boiling water for shaves in desert camps between Benghazi and El Alamein. Although he had studied no geography, he could tell you accurately the distance from Benghazi to Tobruk, along with a description of the topography.

In 1942, he was reassigned to the 5th Indian Division and moved east with them through Cyprus, Persia, and finally into Burma.

His payment came from the men themselves: 10 annas a month from the soldiers, while officers paid as much as they liked. At Pegu, he told stories as he worked. He would trim the edges of a moustache with care, stopping only to make a point with the comb. His audience, whether sepoy or major, listened carefully.

"I am proud to belong to this Division," he told me one evening, wiping sweat from his brow with the same cloth he used to wipe his mirror. "We are the best, and I hope to serve here as long as I live." There was no doubt he meant it.

While men like Shah Mohamed worked quietly behind the lines, others were fighting hard a few miles away, as the front moved southward through monsoon and mosquitos. Pegu, the old gateway to Rangoon, loomed next in the long geography of violence.

The Fall of Pegu

Indian troops from the same formation that had fought rear-guard action during the 1942 Burma retreat have now captured Pegu. The Japanese still hold parts of the southern town as of this morning. An assault is underway.

Until last evening, the Japanese were resisting fiercely with machine guns but the crack came this morning with a Japanic suddenness. After blowing off a portion of the bridge over the river which splits the town in two, the enemy removed several of their guns at about midnight to the railway station area where the fighting is now taking place.

Gurkha and Baluchi units were the first to enter the town. In one overnight engagement, a Gurkha platoon killed nearly

37 Japanese soldiers and captured five guns. The advance on the bridge was led by Jemadar Lalbahadur Limbu of East Nepal. Under sustained machine-gun fire, he moved his men forward and personally accounted for a significant number of enemy casualties.

With Pegu fallen, Japanese retreat routes in the south were rapidly disappearing. Roads, river crossings, and bridges were either occupied by our forces or monitored by scouts. Cut off from supply and facing imminent starvation, enemy troops faced encirclement with little hope of escape. The enemy melted into jungle and swamp, pursued by death, much of it at our hands.

Nowhere to Run, South of Pegu (May 1945)

Six Indian Divisions have closed the rat-trap around the Japanese in Burma. Dark heavy monsoon clouds hang low over Southern Burma and every peal of thunder strikes the death-knell of the 15,000 Japanese who had once hoped to march to Delhi!.

Our troops sit and wait but extensive patrolling goes on both by day and night. The patrols return after killing four or five Japanese and on occasions with a few prisoners. More than that is the information that these patrols flash back on their wireless.

"Hello, Dog, Hello, Dog, Wolf calling Wolf calling 400 Japs in the nullah to the east of point 12488 with few LMGs, Over" is the message received at their HQ in an instant.

Within five minutes, an artillery observation post and an RAF visual control panel get busy on the job. And then one hears the pounding of shells and the peals of the airstrike. Next one sees dense clouds of smoke and fire rise from the ground to intermingle with the low watery clouds. The RAF pilots who strafe and bomb are doing a magnificent job unimpeded by the thick clouds and are always quick to the call.

The Japanese are not idle. They are actively probing an escape route across the trunk-road into Moulmein and Indo-China but our troops have screened every way of exit and every track is under continuous observation.

As every day passes with a marked increase in the intensity of the monsoon, a big clash with our forces is likely to occur very soon as the enemy makes a desperate effort to join his comrades near Moulmein and beyond.

With 150 inches of rain during the next five months and no protection malaria and very much short of food and ammunition, his continuance in Burma presents a dark and dismal picture to him. Hence he would make an all-out effort to get out.

At present, the Japanese are mostly in the forests. Some live in villages either ejecting the villagers or removing their bashas to make their own elsewhere. They raid and loot for food and clothing.

The Burmese guerillas take reprisals.

The interior is where the Japanese are is already inundated and a senior Japanese officer is reported as being carried by his men in a sedan chair! Very soon he may be floating, either dead or alive!

This is the present phase of the war in Burma and the fate of these trapped Japanese will be decided in the next few weeks.

War allows no respite. The monsoon was rising behind us, with Rangoon still ahead. Every column pressed on, racing against the sky.

The Race to Rangoon

From Hlegu (@2 in *Battle Narrative Map: The Road to Rangoon*) to the outskirts of Rangoon (@3), Indian cavalry led by the 37-year-old Lieutenant Colonel J. N. Chaudhuri,* O.B.E., of the 16th Light Cavalry, advanced like a swift tide. His regiment, comprising Stuart tanks, Sherman squadrons, Rajput infantry, and British artillery, neutralized 756 mines across 34 miles in four days. The

---

*He later became, as General Chaudhuri, Chief of Army Staff of the Indian Army (1962–1966).

advance was relentless. "Rangoon" was the unspoken password on everyone's lips.

Though another force ultimately entered the city first, the Japanese retreat had been forced by this dashing pursuit. At Milestone 32, engineers of the Madras Sappers cleared over 500 mines in 8 miles, including buried 250- and 500-pound aerial bombs. Bridges were blown, but new Bailey bridges followed swiftly.

The units commanded by Lieutenant-Colonel Chaudhuri demonstrate a feat of great leadership and coordination: one regiment of armored cars of the 16th Light Cavalry, one squadron of the Stuart tanks of the 7th Light Cavalry, one squadron of Sherman tanks of the 5th Probyn's Horse, one company of a battalion of the 7th Rajput Regiment, a battery of self-propelled guns of the British 18th Field Regiment, two sections of the Madras Sappers and Miners, a visual control panel of the R.A.F. and a section of an advance dressing station.

"The success achieved would not have been possible but for the magnificent cooperation of both the Indian and British troops under my command," Lieutenant Colonel Chaudhuri told me, describing the part played by every unit.

The admiration of the commander and his men are mutual. "We couldn't have had a better commander, a better time or a better deal," said Captain E.W. Penny of Childwal,

Lancashire. His Indian second-in-command summed it up in a few brief words: "The finest leader I have ever worked under." Lt. Col. Chaudhuri has a joke to offer everyone he meets from the highest officer to a private soldier but does not tolerate even the least inefficiency!

General J.N. Chaudhuri

At Hlegu, Gurkhas and British troops from Rangoon linked up across a blown bridge, greeting each other by raft. Their unity marked the capture of Burma's main artery, the Mandalay–Rangoon road, just in time as the monsoon began its full onslaught.

In a jungle clearing nearby, a lone platoon of Gurkhas crossed a broken bridge under fire using only girders. They established a bridgehead. The Japanese withdrew, leaving four dead and an LMG behind.

Behind them, further north, Indian artillery gun-trains mounted on open wagons fired daily across the Sittang River from Nyaunglabin. Wireless contact, quick surveying, and patient targeting allowed them to shell Japanese positions with precision. Patrols crossed the river to count the kill. The enemy, pushed from the Pegu Yomas, drifted eastward, harried by jungle, floodwaters, and the constant threat of fire from the sky.

Rangoon was captured on May 2 in an assault from the sea by the Indian 26th Division. By then, however the Japanese had fled the city. There were celebrations all around, all well-deserved.

Lieutenant General Frank Messervy, Commander of the 4th Corps, visiting troops of the 17th Indian Division on a two-day tour, congratulated them on the victory they had achieved in Burma.

"This Division has played the leading part in the advance from the Irrawaddy onwards and has played the foremost part

in the capture of Rangoon," he declared. To Indian troops, he spoke in Hindustani: "Tumari mehnat aur bahaduri se Burma pakadliya" (It is your hard work and bravery that has captured Burma). With typical humor, he announced right then the 14th Army's leave scheme for Indian troops which was received with cheers. He added that he himself had not been home for seven years, and hadn't seen his family for five years and that he was neither going home nor taking leave till the Japanese were completely defeated. Quoting the words of a jawan: "Kala billi chua zarur khayinge" (The Black Cat will surely eat the Jap rats[1]), he exhorted them to be ready for the next onslaught on the fascists of the east.

Jagaddipendra Narayan with PRS Mani

As the campaign neared its conclusion, it entered a new, somber phase of recovery, reflection, and accounting for the human cost. Attention shifted from the battlefield to the wounded and those who tended them. Amid the wounded lay men whose quiet bravery outshone the pageantry of victory.

A Prince Among the Wounded

Captain Jagaddipendra Narayan, Maharaja of Cooch Behar, walked slowly through the wards of Rangoon's military hospital. He paused beside beds, asked after wounds, and listened more than he spoke. The nurses stood straighter when he passed, for "Jugs," as he was known to the British, was a strikingly handsome man. He was the brother of the glamorous Princess Gayatri Devi. Stories followed him, of Harrow and Cambridge, of Hollywood starlets, including one he had briefly married, and of his life at the Palace.

We became close friends. He told me that he had once tried to enlist under a false name, years earlier, and had been turned away. Now things were different. His princely state had supplied men and resources for the campaign.

While wards filled and a prince and other dignitaries walked the rows of the wounded, divisional clerks were already compiling returns: tallies of enemy dead, captured guns and vehicles, and the stores recovered from the field. For those who wage war from a distance, progress is measured in numbers; for those who fight it, the unreckonable measure is loss.

What Was Left Behind (June 1945)

Final divisional returns were posted to HQ. Between December and March, the 20th Indian Division had accounted for 3,024 enemy dead. Captured materiel included:

13 medium machine guns

50 artillery pieces (9 of them 150 mm)

16 tanks

Over 60 motor transports

25 outboard motors

Hundreds of rifles, mortars, and signal sets

Additional recoveries included surgical gloves, 75 mm shells, animal feed, parade boots, and stacks of signaling flags.

Results for the second quarter weren't as yet available.

Recognition followed. One Victoria Cross, awarded posthumously to Fazl Din of the 10th Baluch, marked the campaign's cost. Two CBEs, 6 OBEs, 11 DSOs, 87 Military Crosses, and 129 Military Medals were recorded.

Over 400 men were Mentioned in Dispatches. Subedar Mohd. Fazal and Lance Naik Vir Singh were personally commended by General Slim.

Two months later,* word of Japan's surrender reached us. There was celebration in the streets, but it felt curiously distant, and almost hard to believe the war was over!

Jubilation in Rangoon (August 15, 1945)

Troops of the 5th Indian Division were wild with joy on hearing the news of the unconditional surrender of the Japanese.

Supported by the same black-bereted Indian tankmen who fought alongside them on the drive to Rangoon, Indian and British troops of this senior Indian Division, went round the streets of the city shouting and waving with joy. Their commander, Maj-Gen. Mansergh spoke briefly and to-the-point: "My feeling is not one of relief but of satisfaction. I am particularly glad that my Division has taken a full share and played a gallant part in the victory over the Japanese."

---

*PRS Mani was back in India in the intervening month of July, but not on vacation. Among other activities, he reported from Cuttack, Orissa, on the first graduation function of Utkal University's Indian Air Training Corps.

The 5th has the unique record in the Indian Army of having fought all the Axis partners; they smashed the Italians in Abyssinia, the Germans and Italians in North Africa and the Japanese in Assam, Arakan and elsewhere in Burma. Hence they rejoice doubly at the final liquidation of the Axis.

Among the soldiers was Subedar Major Ganpat Singh, from Pempura village in Jodhpur State. Twenty-eight years in uniform, bearer of the Order of British India, he stood beside his men and spoke quietly: "We rejoice at the news because our people at home will get more of the necessities of life. It would also mean that we could return to our homes and rest, which we need badly."

Others I spoke to echoed similar thoughts of home. Subedar Latif Khan of Kriplian village, Hazara district, recipient of the Indian Distinguished Service Medal, offered his thoughts with deliberation: "First and foremost, I rejoice in our victory over the enemy. Second, it will mean better days at home."

Havildar Mohammad Akbar, Military Medal, from Nahesar in Rawalpindi, drily observed: "It will mean the saving of many thousands of lives."

Army clerks, cooks, sweepers and barbers—all those who never are in the limelight or win honors and awards—were equally proud and enthusiastic over this great victory,

Yet every victory casts its own shadow. Within two years, there would be new borders. We Indians would face a bloody and largely British-imposed partition within two years, tearing us apart, and Burma would experience its own trials for generations. As for me, I was headed into even more of a bloodbath, one that would lead to a change of attitude and career.

Burma was behind us now, but ahead lay the Malayan coast, and the road to Singapore, where we planned to celebrate the Japanese surrender. But for the moment, the Black Cats had reached the sea.

7

Singapore Liberated[1]

September 1945

The Allied landing at Singapore re-established British authority, formalized Japanese surrender, and initiated the massive undertaking of liberating and repatriating thousands of prisoners of war.

The long road through Burma and Malaya had finally led us to the gates of Singapore. For weeks we had imagined this moment of the return to the island where our comrades had been forced to surrender three and a half years earlier. Now, in the heavy heat, we watched the city stir awake from occupation. The Union Jack was to rise again, prisoners to be found and freed, and the victors to meet the vanquished. Fragments of joy, disbelief, and duty were stitched together into the strange peace that follows war.

Punjabis Hoist Union Jack, September 6

I watched our heroes march up the slope to Government House, their boots ringing on the stone steps still scarred by shell fragments. The sight felt both unreal and inevitable.

Government House, Singapore, was the venue of a picturesque ceremony this afternoon when the Punjabis hoisted the Union Jack over it. I couldn't help chuckling, though, as they had trouble finding the British flag. After searching for an hour, a local Chinese school gave them one.

Lieutenant Colonel Sarbjit Singh Kalha, DSO, commanding the 2nd Battalion of the 1st Punjab Regiment, marched his troops in and mounted the guard. The Chinese dragon crests on their berets were glittering in the midday sun as they stepped smartly, proud of the achievements of the Indian Army. It was like a peacetime guard mounting, and the Punjabis in their olive-green battledress, which seem to glitter like gold in the Singapore sun, clearly enjoyed it after many years of war. The ceremony was perfect except for the absence of a band.

The 2nd Battalion of the 1st Punjab Regiment, nearly 160 years old and first raised in 1781 as the 6th Native Infantry, has a proud and storied history. They first distinguished themselves in the China War of 1842, where they suffered more from the jungle's dragons than the enemy—and ever since, the dragon has been their regimental crest. After campaigns in Mesopotamia and on the Northwest Frontier, they fought in World War II across Arakan, Imphal, and Burma. They first met the Japanese at Donbaik, held out against overwhelming attacks, and later helped relieve the 7th Indian Division by capturing key heights in the Ngakyedauk Pass. They went on to defend at Imphal and spearhead advances along the Tiddim Road, where Subedar Ramsarup Singh earned a posthumous Victoria Cross for capturing Kennedy Peak. All in all, they had won 115 awards for bravery.

While the Union Jack fluttered again over Government House, just beyond the city's outskirts the first encounters between the free and the freed were taking place; quieter, more human proofs that the war had truly ended.

POWs Re-Unite, September 6

Two men from Leicester were overjoyed to meet for the first time outside a prisoner-of-war camp in Singapore.

After three years of mental weariness, sickness, and toil as a prisoner in Japanese hands, Aircraftsman Dennis Lacey, of 166 Brunswick Street, Leicester, jumped with joy when accosted by Fusilier Cyril Snutch of Main Street, Saddington.

Fusilier Snutch was marching along with Punjabi troops of occupation when they reached a POW camp. Snutch looked at a weak figure leaning on a post of the barbed-wire fence, hesitated for a moment, and then advanced to ask his hometown.

As the low reply "Leicester" came, both shook hands vigorously, and a volley of questions and answers followed.

"For three years the Japs forced me to work cutting stones on hills, and my health broke down owing to poor nourishment," said Lacey to me. "But since our troops came, I am improving and being taken care of. I hope to be on my way home soon."

Next to him, another Australian prisoner hailed "Johnny!" to a Gurkha and questioned him. "Gurkha?" he asked. "Ji," replied the stocky Nepalese, and immediately they shook hands and embraced each other.

There were similar encounters throughout the city. Two first cousins from Fontwell, Sussex, had a joyful reunion after 24 years when they met outside a POW camp. Major Allen Robinson of the 9th Gurkha Rifles had been interned by the enemy. His cousin, Lieutenant Kenneth Robinson of the Royal Artillery, serving in Singapore as a Japanese interpreter with the occupation forces, located the major at the Changi Camp. He brought him news of his family, which the Major was delighted to hear.

"I saw him when I was five years old and could not easily recognize him," Lieutenant Robinson told me. "He has just missed seeing his brother, Captain Michael Robinson of the Royal Army Ordnance Corps, who left India only two months ago for repatriation. I knew he was somewhere in Malaya, since we had received a Red Cross card from him, but I never hoped to meet him so soon. It is difficult to describe how happy we are. I'm very glad I came to Singapore."

As we moved from the joy of reunion to the practicalities of occupation, the work of restoring order began.

Occupation and Recovery, September 8

General Auchinleck's Punjabis have occupied the northwest area of the Singapore Naval Base, where they found all equipment and ack-ack guns well-greased and the breeches clean. As per agreement, Japanese naval personnel were not disarmed. Sikhs are guarding a wireless station where 12 Japanese operators are still in communication with their headquarters.

The Cantonment Bridge has a combined services defense—the Hazariwals guard the western end and naval ratings (non-commissioned sailors) the other, from where commences the zone occupied by the Navy.

At a Japanese medical headquarters in the base, when one of our officers gave the Japanese officer notice to vacate in two hours, the latter was more than surprised and blinked for a few minutes after looking at his watch, which already showed seven. It was then explained to him that his was Tokyo time and that it was only four by our time. As I walked through the echoing room, their charts were still pinned to the walls, their medical equipment arranged neatly as if for inspection.

The place was vacated half an hour earlier than required. After three years of fighting in the jungles, this First Battalion of the First Punjab Regiment is now enjoying the comforts of electric lights, fans, beds, hot water, clean clothes, and clear air.

The most bittersweet task was sending home those who had endured captivity.

Gurkha and Service Corps Evacuation (Singapore, September 8, 1945)

Among the 2,000 Indian ex-prisoners of war who are being evacuated to India by sea tomorrow and the day after, a large proportion are Gurkhas, most of whom have not been to Nepal for nearly seven years. Gurkhas in the Indian Army go on leave to their homeland only once in three years owing to the long and arduous journey.

Their port of call is Madras, where extensive arrangements for their reception have been made. The others of the party are mostly from the Service Corps.

The sick had first priority; there were 900 bedridden cases travelling in the two hospital ships *Karoa* and *Amarapura*. So many were suffering from the effects of malnutrition, thanks to the Japanese. They were cared for on the ambulance ship *Rajula*, and the troop ships *Risaldar Ekma*, *Dilaura*, and *Devonshire*. I knew that some of the men on board might not survive the journey.

British officers of the Indian Army were also travelling, 90 percent of whom had elected to go to India first in the company of their men.

Even as ships filled with the returning, new faces arrived. At the end of war, leaders always come to honor those who have fought, and to transfer power. The latter, of course, is what the British were fighting for.

Lord Mountbatten's Tribute to Indian Troops, September 11

On the eve of Victory Day at Singapore, at a crowded press conference in Government House, Lord Louis Mountbatten, Supreme Allied Commander, South East Asia, paid glowing tributes to the Indian troops under his command.

"Indian troops have formed the largest part of our ground forces," he said. "They have fought in every big victory and deserve the highest praise.... We couldn't have better fighting troops."

Listening to him, I thought of the barefoot but cheerful soldiers I had seen crossing the Irrawaddy only months ago. Many were here with us now, sharing in this great moment. Looking at the shining faces of our troops, I hoped that his words about us would never be forgotten.

Mountbatten also disclosed that the greatest tribute to the 14th Army came from General Heitarō Kimura, Commander of the Japanese Army in Burma, who declared:

"I beg to inform Your Excellency that I have passed the ceasefire order for the whole of the Burma area army. If Your Excellency can inform me where my troops are, I shall more easily inform them of the ceasefire order."

Mountbatten spoke, too, of the enormous scope of British South East Asia Command's (SEAC) responsibilities—1.5 million square miles, with 128 million people—and of the immense task of rehabilitation now that the fighting had ceased.

Lord Mountbatten gives a public address from the steps of the Municipal Buildings in Singapore during the surrender ceremony on September 12, 1945. To the left of Mountbatten are Admiral Power and Lieutenant General Slim, and to the right Lieutenant General Wheeler and Air Chief Marshal Sir Keith Park[2]

The next day, his words found their echo in the Municipal Building, where the formal surrender unfolded before the world.

Japanese Surrender Ceremony, September 12

General Itagaki, with credentials and seal from Field Marshal Count Terauchi, surrendered in person to Lord Mountbatten, Supreme Allied Commander, South East Asia.

Brigadier K.S. Thimayya, Captain Jagaddipendra Narayan, Maharaja of Cooch Behar, and Lieutenant Colonel Sher Ali represented the Indian Army and States. The honor done to these three officers was in recognition of the part played by Indian troops in the defeat of the Japanese in Southeast Asia.

The Padang was crowded since early morning; the Dogras presented the guard of honor, while Punjabis, Gurkhas, and Madrasis were also on parade.

General Itagaki signed eleven copies of the document, stamping each with the seal of Count Terauchi and his own. Every copy was countersigned by Lord Louis, who then appeared on the steps and proclaimed the Allied military occupation. The Union Jack was unfurled; the anthems of Britain, America, China, and the Netherlands were played by the Royal Marines.

The ex-Indian POWs, compelled in 1942 to attend the Japanese triumph, now came freely to cheer. "We were forced to be present at a similar function the Japs held in

1942," said a group of Chinese, "but today we all came voluntarily to take part and cheer."

For the thousands who had suffered under the Japanese, that day's pomp gave way to quieter celebrations in the streets. In the days that followed, joy spilled through the streets. Men were shipped home, under varied states of health, and with them went the last breath of war.

The Joy of Repatriation, September 14

Nine days after the first troops landed on the island, there was still cheering in the streets of Singapore. Convoys moved constantly to the harbor carrying hundreds of Indian ex-prisoners of war on their way home. The gratitude in the men's eyes spoke volumes.

While spending up to four years behind barbed wire, many doubted they would ever return home. They had not expected that their fellow-soldiers, who had risen to fame for their deeds in Africa, the Middle East, and Europe, would arrive to liberate them. They embraced us warmly in Indian fashion, heart to heart. Their joy doubled as food, clothing, and medicine arrived like manna from the skies. They thanked us profusely for remembering them during their days of captivity, and their faces brightened up as we told them our plans for repatriating them to India.

One Punjabi jawan, emaciated but bright-eyed, told me that five years earlier, as the red hue of the setting sun cast long shadows near the village well, he had bidden goodbye to his young wife. He had now sent word that he would see her again soon. Others asked what the cities of India looked like now, and how their people had borne the war.

When the homeward journey began, these brave soldiers waved and cheered. Yet, when the lines of defeated Japanese marched past toward their detainment areas, they jeered loudly. It was a brief venting of long years of pain.

Yet not all was ceremony and return. Across the island, old enemies were being disarmed and new duties begun.

When Japanese guards at the Sembawang airstrip allowed civilians to loot stores, Indian prisoners—Mysore Infantry, Punjabis, and Bengal Sappers—disarmed the guards and took over protection of the strip. Major Mir Sarfaraz Hussain led the operation; it was later ratified and commended by senior Allied officers.

Guarded by a detachment of Jats, 20 Japanese military police officers were marched 6 miles in the heat to Pearl Hill Jail. As they passed their former headquarters, they stared silently at the building once dreaded by the city. Two Indian jawans, Sepoy Amilal and Naik Mahsud Ali of the 3/9 Jat Regiment, led the escort. They were innocent representatives of an Army that now stood as an occupying power.

Among those marching out of barracks and airfields were Indian men who had once fought under the Japanese flag: INA volunteers now disarmed, their loyalties still debated. For the regular troops, many of whom had fought them in Burma, their presence stirred an eerie silence.[3]

For days, the ceremonies and logistics continued. Victory felt absolute, yet beyond the parades stood unresolved questions. For even as Allied officers accepted the surrender, the INA trials loomed ahead, forcing the Empire to defend not just its victory, but its right to have commanded at all.

The Japanese had surrendered, and guns were silent. Yet even in victory, the weight of memory lingered in my mind, overflowing with images of comrades lost and of the long and glorious journey from the Manipur mountains across Burma to this port city. It was thanks to our valiant troops that India had been saved, and Burma and Malaya liberated. It was also a relief to see POWs freed, and the INA disarmed. The war was indeed over, but Mother India was facing a new and very severe challenge as it sought its freedom. As for me, I was shipped with the SEAC to report on yet another conflict. This time it was in Java, where I was to face my own reckoning.

Lord Mountbatten inspects the 17th Dogra Regiment in Singapore on September 12, 1945[4]

Japanese soldiers executing Indian POWs in Singapore in 1942[5]

8

Java Security Operations[1]

September–October 1945

As Indonesian nationalism explodes into open revolt, Allied troops entering Java face collapsing Japanese authority, Dutch ambitions, and violent street uprisings.

Born and growing up in times of revolutions, I was fascinated with the accounts of the struggles led by Garibaldi and Bolivar. The contemporary non-violent revolution of Mahatma Gandhi stirred my patriotism deeply but it did not seem adventurous enough to evoke active response in me. My appetite for participating in a revolution in foreign lands in the image of my heroes remained unsatisfied. As a war correspondent, even after the sufferings witnessed and endured along the way, I was actually thrilled when destiny took me to Indonesia in September 1945 when the country was in the throes of a revolution.

Like any good journalist, I had brushed up on the history of Indonesia's recent past in order to understand what was happening in Indonesia. By March 9, 1942, while I was working at AIR in Delhi, the Japanese had occupied Java, replacing 300 years of Dutch rule. There was little resistance from the demoralized Dutch, following Hitler's occupation of their homeland.

According to the *Djojobojo Prophecies* of the 12th-century King Jayabaya, the Javanese Nostradamus, white men would rule over Java for many long years, until they would be driven out by a "yellow race from the North." These "yellow dwarves" would remain for three and a half years, after which Java would become free. To most Javanese, the arrival of the Japanese seemed the fulfilment of the prophecy.

History is shaped by individuals. I came to know in person Indonesia's extraordinary trio of leaders Sukarno, Hatta, and Sjahrir. They had different relationships with the Japanese under occupation. The rulers had envisaged the setting up of an Indonesian government as they had done in Burma, with control in Japanese hands.

The Japanese first tried to utilize feudal and religious elements for support, but when this failed, they turned to Sukarno and Hatta to execute their vision. As the harshness of the Japanese regime became increasingly evident, the Sukarno–Hatta combine acted as a buffer while simultaneously disabusing the people of any faith in the Japanese as their liberators, stirring their zeal for freedom.

In a secret meeting at Hatta's residence, the three leaders agreed that while Sukarno and Hatta would cooperate with the Japanese and insulate the administrative machinery from excessive interference by the Japanese Army (the "collaborationist" camp), they would allow Sjahrir's underground resistance to operate separately.

By 1943, as the war turned, Japan mobilized over a million Indonesians into various militia, unwittingly providing a trained revolutionary army. The occupation meanwhile brought forced labor and starvation, strengthening nationalist feeling and resulting in more youth unrest. Following Japanese Premier Kuniaki Koiso's October 1944 promise of independence, Sukarno and Hatta were allowed to act more openly.On March 1, 1945, a Preparatory Committee for Independence was formed to consider constitutional and economic issues.

After Japan's surrender on August 15, 1945, Sukarno and Hatta were kidnapped by a youth committee to press for independence. Admiral Tadashi Maeda, a Japanese navy officer sympathetic to the nationalist cause, secured their return, and on August 17, 1945, Sukarno and Hatta declared Indonesia's independence.

Once he had made the proclamation, Sukarno ordered all Japanese flags on public buildings to be replaced by the Indonesian red and white. In the few cases where Japanese and their troops resisted these orders, the masses turned extremely violent and massacred them. Otherwise, the disarming and internment of the Japanese troops (a task that came to be finally allotted to Mountbatten's SEAC) was carried out peacefully by the Indonesian regulars assisted by the population as well as militias. Most of the Japanese who were quite bewildered by the collapse of the Imperial government and army surrendered to the Indonesians peacefully. The status quo more or less lasted until Allied soldiers arrived, along with me.

En Route to Java, September[2]

Our convoy of landing craft moved southward from Singapore in staggered formation, the vessels spaced just far enough for visibility. The voyage lasted many days and covered 900 miles. The convoy included the Seaforth Highlanders, 1st Patiala Infantry, and 16th Punjab Regiment. It was uneventful, and the troops enjoyed it—particularly the Seaforths, who did not miss the customary "ducking" ceremony while crossing the equator.

Landfall came early in the morning. Java rose low and green on the horizon. It was September 29, 1945, and I had landed at Jakarta's port of Tanjung Priok.

I was well aware that the Dutch aimed to use British and Indian forces to restore control. However, Britain's Lieutenant General Sir Philip Christison, the Allied Commander, recognized Sukarno's government and, following Lord Mountbatten's directives, sought to avoid hostilities. The Dutch quickly raised local forces. In Jakarta, flags and banners fluttered as armed regulars and irregulars patrolled the streets. The civilians remained wary.

Compared with the enthusiastic reception we had in Burma and Singapore, local reaction here has been a little lukewarm owing to strong nationalist feelings among the Indonesians. In Singapore we were received at the docks by cheering crowds who hung festoons all along our way, but here in Batavia only children waved and cheered at us.

To an Indian aware of history, Java brings back memories of Indian colonization in the country in the early centuries—

during the Pallava, Chola, and Gupta periods. The Indian jawans, even if not fully conversant with historical events of that faraway period, still have a vague idea of this ancient connection.

Our soldiers' routine activities continue as usual. They have their morning physical training and parades, and in the evenings they either play volleyball or hockey. As more sports goods become available, the now-empty playing fields in Batavia will once again witness the nimble-footed Indians joyfully playing their national game of hockey. What makes them happiest of all is the mail from home, which has at last begun to arrive regularly.

One striking sight was that of deluxe saloon cars rolling along the streets of Jakarta. Behind the wheels were our drivers, men whose courage had been forged on the heavily mined roads of Burma, now steering these luxury cars with the same precision and skill they had once shown handling trucks and jeeps under fire. The Japanese had neglected most of their cars, but the Indian mechanics, who had been with these drivers throughout the fighting in Burma, were also here, some of them having been mechanics in big garages in India before the war.

The Bengal Sappers—who had lifted mines, disarmed booby traps, and built bridges and roads along the route to Burma—were now in Jakarta doing odd jobs from turning off water taps in officers' messes to printing a small newspaper. They repaired fuses, replaced bulbs, and fixed leaky taps. Every now and then, they received telephone calls from various units asking them to attend to electrical failures, and they rushed to set things right. Another officer would call to say his bathroom was flooded, and again the sappers would arrive with their tools.

Apart from that, the main work consisted of patrolling, escorting European and Eurasian internees and refugees, and guarding hospitals, vital points, and internment camps. In addition to these duties, whenever the peace of the city was disturbed or looting occurred, our detachments were rushed in to maintain law and order.

The peace of the city was in fact often disturbed, for there was a rising anger among the Indonesians.

Vigilante Murders of Japanese, October 5

Eight Japanese bodies—victims of a murder at the Manggarai wireless station four days ago—were exhumed this evening. A Japanese fatigue party, under the direction of a Royal Signals officer, dug only four feet before locating a body. Two bodies in a fairly decomposed state were examined and bore sword wounds on the backs of their necks. The area for hundreds of yards around is permeated with the smell of death.

The wall of a small outhouse facing the entrance to the place bears bullet marks, and a few of the bullets picked from the ground below are quite rusted. According to an Indonesian from the adjoining village, the locals stopped a Japanese truck whose occupants, instead of halting, fired a shot. As a result, a mob of about 500 men chased them with swords and killed them right in front of the wireless station. One Japanese man who escaped was caught a little later and killed in the same way. After burying their victims, the mob went into the station and looted the furniture and equipment.

Indian Troops Open Fire after Killings, October 11

After an armed Indonesian mob attacked and killed a British officer and an Indian Viceroy's Commissioned Officer of a Punjab battalion, Indian troops opened fire that afternoon on the locals and rounded up about 40 Indonesians armed with rifles and dahs. Six wounded Indonesians were brought in for medical attention at the aid post. As far as is known, no locals were killed.

The clash began when shots were fired at a passing truck in the Cornelis area. A British captain with a platoon of Punjabis went to investigate. When he went forward with one section and neared a road junction, he left the section and, accompanied by his jemadar, moved east toward the railway. Near the railway, they were fired upon by small arms, and their bodies were later found mutilated with knives. Immediately, the section and more troops rushed in and opened fire. The area, thickly built with innumerable lanes, was combed before sunset. About 40 Indonesians were arrested, some armed with rifles and dahs. The strength of the armed mob has not yet been estimated.

Indian Troops Attacked at Road Blocks, October 13

Two more incidents occurred yesterday afternoon in which Indian troops had to open fire purely in self-defense against an unruly mob armed with spears and daggers. While on his way to inspect his guards at the KPM Hospital in the Ziekenhuis area, a senior officer of the Patiala Regiment noticed roadblocks of boulders and logs of wood being erected by locals.

Since he did not have enough men with him, he passed them by. On his return from the hospital, he saw six roadblocks manned by a crowd armed with daggers and spears. When requested to clear the barriers, the crowd shouted menacingly and began throwing stones at his vehicle, one of which broke the windscreen and injured him slightly.

As he saw the mob closing in, he ordered them to disperse, but they waved swords and dahs in a threatening manner. After firing one warning shot, he again told them to go away, but when they persisted, he and his men fired three more rounds, killing two and wounding one. The crowd dispersed, and he removed the remaining barriers without further incident.

As he reached a section post, the crowd followed him. They were again told to disperse but maintained a threatening attitude. When they approached closer, the troops fired four shots, after which the crowd finally dispersed. Another patrol of Sikhs on a different road was attacked with spears later that evening and was forced to fire one round, arresting nine men who were manning a roadblock.

Indian troops were once again caught in a bind. They were serving a colonial master with orders to suppress a fellow-Asian people's struggle for independence, one that India had not yet achieved. From the names and other cultural references they ran across, our soldiers knew that it was a country that had strong historical influences from India.

As an embedded reporter, it was my still my job to pursue the truth, and report it to my bosses who would of course censor it. This time, however, the conflicts I felt were decisive.

9

Surabaya Revolt[1]

October–December 1945

The Battle of Surabaya began with clashes in early October 1945 and erupted into full battle on November 10, when about 20,000 Indonesian troops and countless volunteers faced the far better-armed British and Indian forces. Amid Surabaya's chaotic revolt, PRS witnesses the city's descent into open warfare and feels his own loyalties shift as the gulf between occupiers and nationalists widens.

A Cool Welcome, October 25

We landed at Surabaya without incident along with the 49th Indian Infantry Brigade. We travelled on a landing craft from

Batavia; the sea was often rough. The port was "decorated" with anti-Dutch and anti-imperialist slogans, and for the first time in Java, slogans also appeared in Hindustani: Azadi ya Khunrezi (Freedom or Bloodshed).

Its effect on the Indian troops—especially the Mahrattas and Rajputs, who make up this brigade—was remarkable. Reports have reached me that they are already beginning to ask their officers if they have to fight the Indonesians. I had been warned by the Senior General Staff Officer at Batavia to be on guard, as Surabaya is an extremist center.

The locals here don't seem as cordial as those in Batavia. When I produced my passport from the Republican Government and requested the police at the harbor to provide a car to get me to the city, they were reluctant even to answer and sneered at my Malay. I reached Hotel Liberty in the evening in Royal Navy Lt. Tony Cardew's jeep. The route was manned by heavily armed military and police, and many barricades were visible. None of them acknowledged our greetings—they looked suspicious.

In light of recent incidents around Batavia, I think they are beginning to regard us as the vanguard of Dutch imperialism. The pity is that we are all Indians here, and like their leaders in Batavia, we know we have not come to Java of our own volition. We met a few local Indians who warned us to be careful, as they anticipated trouble.

Mallaby's Misjudgment, October 26

The clear and cool morning of October 26 scurried into an oppressive and humid day as the sun rose to its zenith. I heard, or for some reason imagined, the sounds of kettle drums. After coffee, I attended an early press conference with Brigadier A.W.S. Mallaby, commanding the 23rd Indian Division. Brigadier Mallaby was a much decorated soldier of great promise and yet gentleness of heart, and I was shocked to hear him say that he had emphatically told the locals that he was the ruler of the place and they had to obey him. As I confided in my diary:

But alas, it often happens with renowned leaders... Mallaby misjudged the local situation and viewed it in terms of regular forces and equipment—and of firepower! According to one estimate, there had been 15,000 trained Indonesian troops in Surabaya and a much larger number of irregulars armed to wield rifles. He had not taken into account the intense nationalism and mass frenzy. Brigadier Mallaby does not seem to gauge the situation adequately and pooh-poohs the Indonesian strength. Echoes of Glubb Pasha! Playing for*

*The reference is to Lieutenant General John Bagot Glubb, who was commanding the Arab Legion. In the Second World War, he led attacks on Axis–Allied Arab forces. At the time of

time, the usual game... A thousand regrets I am not a free correspondent to report what I observe. Anyway, duty by troops from my country first, and cannot leave them.

Piano Interlude, October 26

As the fierce sun of the day cast its last shadows, the roar and din of the city also whimpered down in gradual protest as swift-moving men and women rushed with aching limbs to their homes for their main meal of the day. At our Hotel Liberty, dinner had long been over and our sentries of the 5th Rajputana Rifles had taken up positions around the building. But I still lingered in the parlor alone, pondering over the events of the day and wondering what lay in store for us. The evening's quiet was occasionally marked by the laughter of the uncaring and hilarious few still drowning the plentiful beer at the bar.

My reverie was jolted when I heard a few bars of *Merdeka* (the Indonesian anthem on freedom) being played on the piano in a distant corner of the parlor. It was little Meena, the manager's 16-year-old daughter. She had quietly slipped in like a cat and as her small fingers danced on the keys, I could see the fervor in her eyes. The song

---

PRS Mani's diary entry, he was already regarded by some Asian nationalists as yet another arrogant imperialist.

convulsed my insides, and I wrote in my diary that night:

Hardly 16, she hypnotizes me with her zeal for the freedom of her country. She speaks only Malay and no English. As I wish her Selamat Malam (Good Night), she pleads with me to take protection during the coming days. Later, as I lie down to sleep, a vague feeling arises that there may be a bloodbath in store for us. Meanwhile, I can hear the other journalists and soldiers still at their beer in the bar!

Air Mail Betrayal, October 27

The next morning the day rose brighter, and I was pleasantly surprised when three members of the Youth Party (Promoeda) called on me. The bearded Jamal, the petite and charming Stri Souchy in her brown batik sarong and soft yellow *kabaya* (blouse-like shirt), and the Balinese Christian girl in her prim blue petticoat and shirt, all of the Promoeda (Youth Wing of the National Movement), met me as instructed by their Information Officer in Batavia.

They offered to take correspondents on a city tour. Ralph Conniston (*New York Times*) and I accepted. We were taken to the police headquarters to be issued permits. As we were leaving the police station, we noticed RAF Spitfires dropping leaflets on the town. Crowds rushed to pick them up, but the police snatched them away.

The Balinese girl, who served as our guide, read a copy and looked grave. I managed to grab one and read it in Malay. Its meaning became quite clear to me. I knew that the proud Indonesians would not surrender their arms, which the leaflet demanded of them. Our guide told us frankly that trouble loomed on the horizon, and after a brief visit to the Antara News Agency Office, deposited us back in our hotel.

Lunch and Aftermath, October 27

Captain Honavar, a colleague from Indian Army Public Relations, and I decided to tramp it out of the hotel to visit some of the Indian merchants in town. T.D. Kundan,[2] who was the President of the local Indian Association, gave us a delicious lunch and briefed us on the situation.

Short-statured and well-educated, Kundan, who had some links with the INA, broadly sympathized with the struggle for Indonesian freedom. Besides moral support, the Indian community also gave generously to Sukarno and his associates. Kundan was an important mediator, much harassed by the intelligence folks in our Field Security Station, and he gave us plenty of information on the local situation. He was a public-spirited man who was keen to avoid armed clashes in Surabaya. As the leader of the 500-strong Indian community in Surabaya, he had ably averted a clash on the first day of our arrival, October 25. Yet, like most of the businessmen from Sind who have spread to remote corners of the world in pursuit of trade, Kundan had a survival instinct based on caution.

Kundan told us that while Sukarno controlled the entire nationalist forces in Surabaya as elsewhere in Java, there were still Communists wishing to go it alone, as well as hot-headed armed irregulars under a young leader of the Robin Hood type named Bung Tomo.

When we finally found our way back to the hotel, we noticed increased activity in town with the Promoeda, armed to the teeth, rushing to various areas and laying roadblocks.

That evening's press conference at Brigade Headquarters was tense. There were grave faces with no smiles. Normally cheerful staff officers Aslam, Chopra, and Singh looked serious. The lid was soon off as we became aware of the ominous portents of a serious battle. Mallaby was posing a calm exterior, though very much perturbed.

Brigadier Mallaby told us that Indonesian Governor Mustafa had fled the town without complying with the promise to cooperate in disarming the population, but Mallaby had been able to take into custody another official promising to carry out the orders. He also said that he informed the locals that he was the ruler of the place and all Indonesians had to accept his authority.

Mallaby did not want us to report how serious the situation was and insisted again on vetting our dispatches. Most correspondents reluctantly agreed. I remained furious that the truth was being suppressed. My diary for the day recorded:

I consider Mallaby's approach as sheer arrogance and left the press briefing sadly disappointed at the inability of our military leaders to avoid incidents. I went back to the hotel and told Honavar for the first time that we were in for trouble and how sorry I felt for the Indian troops. Warriors from North Africa and Burma seem to be forever trapped in the web of destiny to which they so pathetically cling.

Little Meena plays again, this time the Moonlight Sonata, and I am reminded of the ancient city of Delhi, the Red Fort, the River Jamuna, and my friends there. The little girl looks sadly into my eyes and pleads with me to leave the hotel and Surabaya at once, but I tell her that I am Indian and will never flee in the face of danger. Honavar butts in and plays a few Indian melodies which stir me even more deeply, and I retire. Perhaps all my fears are imaginary, but why on earth are the Indonesians parading in the armored cars and tanks taken from the Japanese? Maybe tomorrow everything will be quiet.

Hotel Siege and Massacres, October 28

We woke to a morning of uneasy quiet. The clear dawn yielded to a sky of low cloudy patches, as if a hundred fires had been lit in town. The fierce Sun took deliberate peeps through the clouds, as though it resented our presence. Jamal dropped in early morning to apologize for the abrupt cancellation of yesterday's events and promised to take us around as soon as things became quiet.

Honavar and I had once again lunch with Kundan and sat chatting till 4 p.m. before walking back to our hotel. On our way, we heard the first shots of rifle fire, and we knew the peace of the town had been broken.* More shots were heard, and by dusk, we heard the sounds of battle raging. Our Jat platoon of Rajputanas took up positions at the hotel.

By 7 p.m., the gunfire started coming in our direction, but our troops held fire. Major Finlay of the Australian

---

*PRS. remained unaware that on the way back, they were nearly ambushed – and killed – by a gang of Indonesian fighters. As Heather Goodall points out in *Beyond Borders*, Des Alwi (1927–2010), a young nationalist and later a prominent journalist and diplomat, recognized PRS and another journalist and shouting that they were journalists, not British, called off the attack.

Recovery of Allied Prisoners of War and Internees (RAPWI) took over from me.

My PR colleagues—Honavar, Donald, and Irwin—were deployed along with troops, and I was assigned to the command post to monitor Brigade HQ on our radio receiver since we couldn't sent messages out. However, we could hear all the exchanges between HQ and the units. The news was grim, and each of the units was in distress, sending out SOS calls. HQ reported they were themselves surrounded and a fierce battle was on. Some telephone calls did trickle in, and one was from Kundan, urging me to inform HQ that the Indonesians were anxious to call off the fighting. I replied that I had no contact with HQ and could not leave my post and that he should personally approach HQ with a white-flagged escort.

When one of our Jat guards at the door was seriously wounded, our unit opened fire. In a few moments, we suffered two more casualties, and being short of soldiers, we retreated to the attic of the hotel with only 4 Bren guns, 20 rifles, and 10 pistols. Meanwhile, the mob of 400 Indonesians encircling us carried Tommy guns, Brens, machine revolvers, pistols, rifles, Japanese swords, and bamboo spears and sticks.

Our men defended themselves for three hours. They had been at their posts since the previous evening without food and sleep. Four more of our troops were wounded, and two lay dying for lack of medical attention. It was heartbreaking to sit beside a ribboned Rajput hero of Burma who lay dying with an Indonesian bullet in his heart. He exclaimed to me: "*Hum Dutch ke liye kyon marna hai, Sahib*?" *(Why should we die for the Dutch Sir?).*[3]

No help could be expected, as other detachments were in a similar plight. (In one cinema hall where a detachment of Indian troops had been billeted, the entire place was set on fire by Indonesians, resulting in most of our troops being burned alive.)

Four more Jats were wounded and some of the wounded were dying of thirst and for want of medical attention. After two more hours of resistance, and since no help was forthcoming, we decided to give in, and Major Finlay led us down the stairs with a white flag. Our casualties were promptly evacuated in ambulances by the Indonesians, and the rest of us were loaded into trucks, with flashing bayonets directing us, and taken to the Kalisoesoe prison.

As they saw us being thus led away by youth with bayonetted rifles, the ladies of the Indian family residing adjacent to the hotel commenced to wail for our safety. Touched by this typical Indian motherly concern in a foreign land, with the permission of my escort, I bowed to the eldest of the women and assured them that I would soon return to visit them, which I did a few weeks later after our troops had occupied Surabaya.

On our way to the prison in a truck with guards pointing their loaded weapons at us, armed crowds jeered, aimed and waved their weapons menacingly shouting *Merdeka* (Freedom).

Meanwhile, pressed by his own advisers and the Allied HQ in Batavia about the situation in the city, President Sukarno rushed to Surabaya along with Information Minister Sharifuddin, who had considerable influence in the city, especially amongst the Communists.

Sojourn in Prison, October 28

Our six hours in Kalisoesoe prison were quite an experience. Three of us in a small cell were offered rice mixed with foul-smelling meat and black coffee. As some of my colleagues suspected, in a moment of collective paranoia, that the meat was the flesh of our slain comrades, we took only the coffee!*

---

*I remember, when I was still a child, quizzing my father about this incident when he mentioned it. He suggested that the meat in question may have been horseflesh.

Our first experience of a jail threw me into a state of reverie. I had come to Java as a correspondent in uniform, but I was now a prisoner wondering once again which flag I was serving. Just as I was ruminating about how we would be rescued, Minister Amir Sharifuddin (whom I had greatly befriended in Batavia) visited me and said that the entire episode was a tragic mistake on either side. He informed us that Sukarno, who was in the city to restore calm and peace, had ordered our release and we would be returned to the British lines as soon as free communication had been established.

Later in the evening, my Batavia contact Sufiyan Tanjoeng (a relation of Madame Sukarno) appeared with an armed escort and took all the press correspondents and photographers, including PR personnel, to the local Governor's Palace, where an elaborate meal was laid on for us, with the officials offering profuse apologies for what had happened.

Being released did not restore normalcy for me. It only returned us to a city where conflict had already escalated beyond repair.

However, we were not entirely free. We were taken to Hotel Simpang under protective custody for the next four days. The Indonesians thought it was not safe to send us across the lines to the British HQ. Then an effort was made to send us by train to Batavia with an armed escort, but we were halted in the Central Java town of Madiun and were unable to proceed further, as intense fighting had started in Central Java between Indian troops and the Indonesians.

Meanwhile, on the station master's radio in Madiun, the BBC was reporting: "All quiet in Surabaya!" Our train took us back to "quiet" Surabaya and into protective custody.

During this period, we were placed under the charge of a vivacious and colorful freedom fighter, Miss Yetty Zain,* whose family members were already my friends in Batavia. In fact, it was her brother Rustom, waving a Japanese sword in his hand and at the head of the Indonesian irregulars, who had taken us prisoners. He had then shouted *Gurkha Toetoep* (Gurkha, shut up) at me, though he had known me earlier. To most Indonesians, all Indians were Gurkhas.

---

*Yetty Zain (1924–1982), known later as Yetty Rizali Noor, was a nationalist leader from a prominent family. In addition to her brother, Rustom, mentioned by PRS., she also had another brother, Zarin, who later became Indonesian Ambassador to the US. After Independence, Yetty had a career as a professor of dentistry at Trisakti University in Jakarta, while also being a legislator.

Death of Mallaby, October 30

We were still in custody at the Hotel Simpang when Brigadier Mallaby set out on a mission under a white flag to announce the ceasefire and assist stranded Mahratta troops. His vehicle was speeding along the bullet-swept roads when it was intercepted by Indonesian Republican militia near a British outpost. His troops discharged warning shots into the air to scatter the militia, who responded with gunfire. In the gunfire, Mallaby was killed. Kundan was present next to Brigadier Mallaby when the latter was shot, but managed to escape with light injuries.[4]

The aftermath of Mallaby's killing was swift. The British command issued an ultimatum: all armed Indonesian forces in Surabaya were to surrender their weapons by 6 a.m. on November 10. When no surrender came, Major General Mansergh ordered a heavy bombardment from land, sea, and air on known Indonesian concentrations. The 5th Indian Division then fanned out from their base in Surabaya port to attack the city. According to an unofficial estimate there were about 15,000 trained Indonesian troops in the town in addition to several times that number of armed people who knew to handle rifles. On November 12, for the first time, two or three 75 mm guns fired at us from the Indonesian side, along with Indonesian ack-ack and mortars. They became silent as soon as the guns of the Royal Navy responded.

Indian troops remove a barricade put up by Indonesian nationalists in a street in Surabaya[5]

Our casualties remained extremely light while the counting of Indonesian casualties was difficult owing to the fact that the latter remove their dead quickly. Our aircraft on reconnaissance observed Indonesians digging graves in several parts of the town.

Massacres of Chinese Civilians, November 14–17

A grim civilian toll emerged as Chinese delegates approached our commander requesting protection to bury their dead, most of whom they said, were killed by the Indonesians and not by our fire. Over the next few days, more reports of ill-treatment of Chinese nationals by the Indonesians came in and a leading Chinese walked into our lines his pyjama suit having lost the rest of his possessions. Subsequently a large influx of Chinese refugees arrived from the east of the Kali Semampir river. Relief efforts were established, with more Eurasian and Chinese refugees from that area now safe in camps which we set up for them. However, the atrocities continued unabated. Indonesians rounded up half a dozen Chinese residents and burnt them in their houses.

Dutch and Indian Civilian Recoveries, November 19–December 4

At first, Dutch women and children refugees came dribbling into our lines in groups of five and ten. They informed our troops of many more hundreds of women and children in the custody of armed Indonesians beyond our lines and almost on the verge of death due to starvation and the shock of being in the middle of a battlefield. Many of these women were actually rendering medical aid to the Indonesian wounded but these fascist-inspired extremists had no heart for their work and permitted them to starve.

Immediately, Lieutenant Colonel Sarbjit Singh Kalha, DSO, Commander of the 2nd Battalion, 1st Punjab Regiment sent out rescue patrols beyond our lines to fetch them. Our Punjabis displayed the same courage and sacrifices as in Burma when they opened the Ngakyedauk Pass in Arakan.

A 20-year-old Eurasian girl wearing the Red Cross on her arm escorted by one of our soldiers approached our forward company commander Major Mohamed Iqbal, of Kalanaur district, Rohtak. She pleaded with him for the rescue of her comrades several of whom were sick and wounded, or starving. The Punjabis went in despite booby traps and snipers and gradually brought back these women and children. The Punjabis had to either shoot down their Indonesian guards or disarm them but they mostly ran away. On one day alone, the Punjabis rescued nearly 400 women and children from the hands of the Indonesian extremists.

"We owe our lives to the Indian troops," the girl told me. "But for them we must have been dying a gradual death in Indonesian hands."

She was born and bred in Surabaya but now the extremists have made her homeless and a refuge along with her aged parents.

The men volunteered with all their rations to feed the refugees immediately and between mouthfuls of the manna that had been brought to them by the Punjabis, these women were ecstatic with joy relief and thankfulness. Little children with biscuits in their hands came and looked up with admiration at the tall Punjabis and though language separated them their eyes expressed gratitude. More than any honors of war, the Punjabis consider it equally high honor to be soldiers in the service of humanity.

While a small percentage of Indians left Surabaya for Singapore before November 9, most of them remained behind to look after their shops and homes. In the first few days of our advance we brought under protection about 100 of them. However, those living in the center of the town had concentrated themselves together in the Coen Boulevard in the Darmo area. On November 27, the Punjabis and Dogras advanced into Darmo and rescued 75 Indians including women and children. They told me that the Indonesians treated them well.

Bravery Under Fire, November 24–December 4

November 21. An outstanding patrol yesterday morning by men of the 1st Madras Regiment located an ack-ack gun position being set up by the Indonesians to the west of the airstrip seriously threatening our use of the airstrip. This patrol under Jemadar P.R.K. Rama Rao of Coconada town East Godavari district Madras Province brought back accurate information about the gun position and immediately our planes strafed and bombed the area. In the afternoon on his way to investigate the results of the bombing he and his platoon were ambushed by nearly 200 armed Indonesians. The Indonesian ambush consists of laying tree trunks along the road and crowding near there on the approach of our troops. The unruly noises they make is quite predominant on such occasions. Jemadar Rao and his men killed 15 Indonesians and returned to his base without suffering any casualties.

November 24. Prompt and bold action by a Dogra Naik averted a serious situation for the 1st Dogra Regiment while they were advancing along the west bank of the River Kalimas on Thursday. Since we had no troops on the east bank the Dogras were exposed to fire from the Indonesian guns on the other bank. One of our machine gun posts on the water's edge was covering our advance along a bridge held by us. When its first gunner was wounded severely and a second gunner on his way to take over was also wounded fatally Lance Naik Faquir Chand Dogra, Rajput of village Naror district, Undampur, in change of the gun section rushed out of cover and exposing himself to more than 20 yards swept by machine gun fire brought back the wounded first gunner to safety. Then once again daunting the 20 yards of fire he manned the machine gun post and silenced the Indonesian gun by killing its entire crew. But for his prompt and bold action our advance would have been held up causing us quite heavy casualties.

December 4. Former swimming champion of Cochin, South India, Major C.P. Ayyappa Menon, 1st Madras Regiment, has added a Surabaya achievement to his swimming career. In recent operations commanding a company of Madrasis on the north bank of the Wonokromo Canal, he and his men were fired upon with mortars and machine guns by the Indonesians on the opposite bank. The canal was 30 yards wide and the only boat was lying on the Indonesian side. On his own initiative and acting with quick decision, Major Menon asked his men to give him covering fire and plunged into the canal. Dodging and ducking mortars and machine gun and sniper fire, he brought the boat safely to his own bank. Within a few minutes with a section of his men he crossed the canal in the boat and cleared the village.

"It was exciting and it was my first swim under fire," Major Menon told me.

Most of the fighting was now done. We suffered nearly 300 British and Indian casualties whereas the Indonesians lost more than 7,000, according to estimates.

Looking back, the Battle of Surabaya was clearly an aberration. Indonesian extremism and needless British provocation contributed to the violence. It served as a crucible for young revolutionaries, including the Indonesian Communists. The British made matters much worse with punitive assaults by air, sea, and land.

Jat Bren gunners in Surabaya, November 15, 1945[6]

In 1946, I resigned my Army commission in protest against the Allied atrocities in Surabaya. I returned to Java later that year, not in uniform, but with a press card from both the *Free Press Journal* of Bombay and the Indonesian ANTARA news agency. My loyalties had shifted, from duty to the British to a support for nationalist movements not only in India and Indonesia, but in other Asian countries emerging from colonial oppression. Surabaya taught me that.

But what of the loyalties of other Indian soldiers? Our Indian soldiers' experience with British military leaders over nearly a 150 years had developed in them a strong sense of duty to that leadership. As veterans of the Second World War, they had fully imbibed the spirit of the Allied cause in fighting the German and Japanese powers.

However, I could also see there was considerable sympathy among Indian troops for Indonesians. Our troops were conversant with the developments in India, the parleys between Indian nationalist leaders and British statesmen and the prospect of a free India in the future. Compared to their earlier goal of defeating the Japanese, they were not particularly enthusiastic about their current mission. Nevertheless, our troops were disciplined and for the most part, acted with a strong sense of duty to the

British authority to whom their loyalty was pledged. The British, in turn, utilized the Indians under their command though they were quite aware where the sympathies of the troops lay.

The Indian troops in Indonesia were mostly Punjabis, Madrasis, Rajputs, Mahrattas, and Pathans and belonged to the Hindu, Muslim, and Christian religions. While all of them resented their role in Indonesia, the Muslim amongst them were especially perturbed. About 600 of them deserted—allegedly enticed, as the British said, while admitting that some of them did not like to fight the Indonesians. Later, in Jogjakarta, I met them often in the spacious lounges of Hotel Merdeka, as well as in their camps, and several fronts. Greeting me with a *Jai Hind* or *Azad Hind*, they always behaved with dignity, and the only desire they expressed to me was that India should be told the truth about them.[7] They were well-spoken of by Indonesian officers. Undoubtedly, some had been lured, as the British claimed, by material benefits. A few also gave their lives to the cause of Indonesia.[8]

I stayed on in Java until 1949. By then, as a diplomat, I was serving the cause of a truly independent India, which was the ultimate honor, one that I will cherish till my dying day.

What I have written here is the only account I know by an Indian officer and correspondent who experienced this particular world of Asian war not from the press box but from deep within.

PRS Mani: A Brief Biography[1]

The character, thoughts, and actions of my father should be clear from his writing in the preceding chapters. While that account covers the 1940s, here are some biographical details to round out the picture of his life.

PRS Mani was born on February 14, 1915, in the town of Chittoor, Madras Presidency (now Andhra Pradesh), into a middle-class Tamil Brahmin joint family. He grew up in the home of his maternal grandfather, B.C. Ragaviah. BCR was a public prosecutor, a member of the Indian National Congress and a leading lawyer in Chittoor. He was given the title of Rao Bahadur by the British but, out of nationalist fervour, avoided using it. PRS's mother, Kunjammal, while still of tender age, married P.R. Krishnan, a graduate of Presidency College, Madras, whose education there was paid for by BCR. Krishnan was employed as a civil servant carrying out school inspections in the Education Service. Kunjammal took on responsibility for managing the household, and as a result, PRS was brought up mainly by his mother's two sisters.

Life for Indians in the early 1900s was hardly easy. Childhood was marked by illness and death. PRS suffered several bouts of malaria before his teens. His older brother came down with polio, and a younger brother had died while very young. He also had a sister who is fifteen years younger and still living.

Nevertheless, their house was rather luxurious by the standards of colonial Indians of the day. They had hand-carved teak furniture and a Phaeton cab with horses. Chittoor was a hot, dry place, and in the evenings, BCR would take PRS out in that vehicle, with the boy dressed in his best, on an excursion to the park, where they would engage in a stroll.

PRS was born during the First World War and was a toddler during the Russian Revolution. From his early years, he became aware of tumultuous historical changes through discussions in the household and in nationalist newspapers like *The Hindu* and *Mathrubumi*, which carried headlines from across the nation and the world. The winds of nationalism blew hard even in Chittoor, and BCR, as a locally prominent Congress man, was in touch with other nationalists in southern India, attending the INC meetings in Madras. Annie Besant, the British suffragette, Home Rule activist, and Theosophist, had earlier visited their home and became friends with BCR. In addition to sharing ideas about the nationalist struggle, Besant taught Theosophical meditation sessions at BCR's home, in a spacious top-floor room made resplendent with coloured glass.

Theosophy, founded by Helena Blavatsky in the late nineteenth century, had become a worldwide movement by the turn of the century. It attracted the Tamil upper caste despite its eccentric spiritualism (with seances, mediums, and the like) as it appeared to affirm aspects of ancient Indian wisdom, aligned with Brahmin-professed values like vegetarianism and temperance. Most of all, Theosophists supported Indian nationalism and Home Rule.

My father studied at the PCR Government High School, Chittoor, an imposing edifice dating back to 1854. He found the school motto "Look Up, Aim High" to be rather inspiring and made it the title of his autobiography. In his own words, he was "not a brilliant student, but very much above average." In 1934, at 19, he joined Madras Christian College at Madras University, where he earned a BA in English in 1937. The College was a major centre for Christianity in India. He then studied law until 1939. During this time, he often visited the Theosophical Society Headquarters in Madras, with its 260-acre Huddleston Gardens on the south bank of the Adyar River.

WHITHER INDIA?

By
JAWAHARLAL NEHRU

A very wonderful book giving lucidly in a few pages the case for Socialism in this country and elsewhere. His exposition of Capitalism as a vicious circle is highly logical as well as equitable. It is the only remedy for the economic crippling of our Motherland even before the influence of Capitalism is felt. Mahamed Ghori could be pardoned but not British Imperialism. The former's

KITABISTAN
ALLAHABAD AND LONDON

raid on the temple of Somnath was with a religious fervour – the latter sapping the Indian Peasantry of their wealth and happiness is highly selfish and typical of the British. Those of our own countrymen who are were and are abetting this crime, stand condemned by their own shame which will come upon them when India becomes energetic.

The vision of Nehru is not far off and those of us who can search their hearts can hear the call even now. It is not by conversion this purpose is going to be achieved but by revolution – not a revolution in blood but a non-violent and very dynamic one taught to us by a great leader of men, Mahatma Gandhi

9th March '39. P.R. Subrahmanyam

PRS Mani's notes (March 1939) on the frontispiece of Nehru's Whither India

In 1939, when my father was just 24, his liner notes on Jawaharlal Nehru's pamphlet *Whither India* left no doubt about his enthusiasm for democratic socialism, especially of the kind that Nehru eventually put in place.

A very wonderful book, giving lucidly, in a few pages, the case for Socialism in this country and elsewhere. His exposition of capitalism as a vicious circle is

> highly logical as well as equitable. It is the only remedy for the economic crippling of our Motherland, even before the influence of capitalism is felt.

As someone taught by British teachers at university, he was particularly blunt about British rule:

> Mohammed Ghazni could be pardoned but not the British. The former's raid on the Temple of Somnath was with a religious fervor – the latter raping the Indian Peasantry of their wealth and happiness is highly selfish and typical of the British. Those of our own countrymen who were and are abetting this crime, stand condemned by their own shame which will come upon them when India becomes energetic.
>
> The vision of India is not far off and those of us who can search their hearts can hear the call even now. It is not by convention that this purpose is going to be achieved but through revolution – not a revolution in blood but a non-violent and very dynamic one taught to me by a great leader of men: Mahatma Gandhi.

In October 1939, PRS was hired by AIR, Madras, as a programme attache and announcer. His first assignment was to survey and report on listeners' reactions to broadcasts from Berlin and Moscow. For that, he had to travel throughout the Madras Province (the new name for the Madras Presidency after 1937). The report got him noticed not only by the AIR establishment in Madras but also received very positively by the controller, Lionel Fieldon, in Delhi. PRS also wrote a script on unemployment, broadcast on the AIR in 1939, called *Bread and Stone*:[2]

> Would you give thy son a piece of stone when he ask for bread? In these days even if you do not beg for bread and starve, stones are hurled at you. The charitable give bread made of stone… That is the lot of the unemployed in this country…
>
> The modern educated youth believes in large scale industries, where he can use his intelligence more than in the monotonous tilling of the soil. That is why there has been little response to this [rural employment] scheme in the Annamalai University. They would rather serve in the Army, for which they are strong enough, than to "go back to the land." Our only hope is that the state will not pursue this policy. This policy is merely a mirage…
>
> The pathos of human suffering is not in the survival of the fittest nor the needy but the survival of the influential. Honesty and merit should play a greater part…

> As unemployed, our hopes are buried in the sand, but like the fabulous phoenix, it is only to rise again... We require a more humane treatment from our fellow-beings.

In February 1940, he was promoted to publicity assistant, working with Victor Paranjothi, the composer of Western music and choirmaster. They became close friends.

While at AIR Madras, PRS also met the great dancer, choreographer and Theosophist, Rukmini Devi Arundale, assisting her with the broadcast of fellow-Theosophist Edwin Arnold's "The Light of Asia," a popular poem about the life of the Buddha.

Rukmini Devi was an extraordinary, self-assured woman, responsible for the revival of Sadiraattam, a classical dance form practised by Dalit women in South Indian temples and suppressed by the British ban on so-called nautch girls. Rukmini gave it the name of Bharatanatyam, or "Indian dance," the name by which it has been known ever since. Thirty-six years old at the time of their meeting, she had already travelled the world promoting the cause of Theosophy and Indian culture with her decades-older husband, George Arundale, the president of the Theosophical Society.

Rukmini became a key influence in PRS's career. Part of their bond came from the fact that her own father was a devoted follower of Annie Besant and Theosophy. Raised by strong women, PRS was especially drawn to Rukmini's self-assured, dynamic personality. In December 1941, he left AIR to take a job as a public relations assistant to Rukmini at her dance and music school, Kalakshetra, in Adyar. Working with her exposed him to stagecraft and public relations. Soon, he was travelling on her behalf all the way to Benares, carrying society documents for safekeeping; many in Madras were worried about the prospect of a Japanese attack on the city (it was briefly bombed by them a year later).

Rukmini Devi also sent him to visit several cities in North India on both Kalakshetra and Theosophical Society work, where she introduced him to key nationalist figures. She also gave him a letter of introduction to her friend Professor Syed Bokhari in Delhi. Bokhari was the head of Broadcasting for AIR and was, of course, aware of PRS's earlier work. He offered him a job at AIR in Delhi as a programme assistant in charge of wartime programmes beamed to Indian residents in Southeast Asia. Rukmini urged him to take up the offer, and so PRS moved to Delhi in February 1942. He worked there at AIR for two years.

Part of PRS's job was to introduce the leading influencers of the time to the audience. One of these figures was Sir Frederick Ernest James, a colonial administrator of India's

Central Legislative Assembly. Mani got to know him well, and one day James suggested he go report on the War. Sir Frederick gave him a letter of introduction to Brigadier Jehu, a former editor of the *Times of India*, asking him to recruit PRS into the Army's Public Relations Department.

The period from 1944 to early 1946 is covered in his writings above, but here is a brief recap of the main chronology. On January 17, 1944, PRS was commissioned and attached to the Public Relations Directorate at the Army GHQ in Delhi. He was 29 at the time.

The freshly commissioned Captain PRS Mani at 29

In April of the same year, he was posted as captain and sent on active service to the then besieged Imphal to "cover," as an Indian Army Observer attached to the 14th Army, the activities of the Indian troops both in action and in the rear. After the Japanese defeat in India, he followed the victorious Indian soldiers in their pursuit of the enemy through Burma, Malaya, and finally Singapore, where he reported on the atmosphere of the Japanese surrender there.

At the end of September 1945, PRS was transferred with the 23rd Indian Division to Batavia, Indonesia. By then, he had learned Malay as well, which came in handy in Indonesia. While in Indonesia, he started an English and romanized Urdu newspaper for troops of the 23rd Indian Division and also radio programmes in Hindustani and Tamil for them. He also renewed his friendship with T.G. Narayanan, whom he had known from AIR and Christian College. Narayanan was *The Hindu*'s war correspondent there, a role different from the embedded journalist that PRS was. Narayanan was conducting a special study of the INA in Southeast Asia, and PRS flew to Calcutta from Jakarta twice to deliver these reports to Sarat Chandra Bose, Netaji's brother, for eventual transmission to Nehru in Allahabad.

After reporting on the events in Surabaya, PRS resigned his army commission in protest against British atrocities there. In early 1946, he became the Singapore and Indonesia correspondent for the *Free Press Journal* of Bombay, and also a reporter for the Indonesian News Agency, ANTARA. While gainfully employed there, he was often in India, where he used to spend his mornings at Nehru's residence at York Road, New Delhi, interacting with Nehru and his family. In addition to having him prepare a daily summary, with clippings, of the Indian newspapers, Nehru encouraged him to liaise with the Indonesian leadership. As a result, PRS helped forge closer relations between Nehru and Sukarno. In April 1946, PRS was instrumental in persuading Indonesian Prime Minister Sjahrir to arrange a shipment of rice (nearly 60,000 tons) to India, where it was sorely needed to prevent yet another famine. It was one of PRS's proudest moments, even though the Dutch bombed the ships carrying the rice.

In October 1947, at Nehru's invitation, PRS interviewed for the Indian Foreign Service (IFS) and was hired as the press attache with the Indian Diplomatic Mission in Jakarta. In January 1949, he was promoted to consul and posted to Jogjakarta, now Yogyakarta.

Saraswathi Mani, Indira Gandhi, and PRS Mani, Stockholm, 1972

After five years in Indonesia, PRS returned to India in 1949 and married my mother, Saraswathi Iyer, who had escaped Burma in 1942 with some of her family.

In February 1950, PRS was appointed deputy chief of Protocol in New Delhi. There followed a sequence of IFS career postings abroad to Manila, Shanghai, Hong Kong, Goa, Bonn, Kathmandu, Colombo (where he was involved in the 1962 peace talks with China), and Mauritius. During those years, my brother Ranjit was born (in 1951), and I arrived in 1955. In 1967, PRS returned to New Delhi, where he first served as a joint secretary (in charge of the Pakistan division) and was later promoted to additional secretary. In 1970, he was posted to Stockholm, where, as ambassador, he served as a delegate to the 1972 United Nations Conference on the Environment, the world's first international conference focused on environmental challenges. He also developed a close friendship with the Nobel Prize-winning economist Gunnar Myrdal, a key voice in welfare-state economics. In 1973, PRS retired from the IFS, but within two years, he was back in a job as special adviser on foreign affairs to the prime minister of Mauritius, where he remained until 1977.

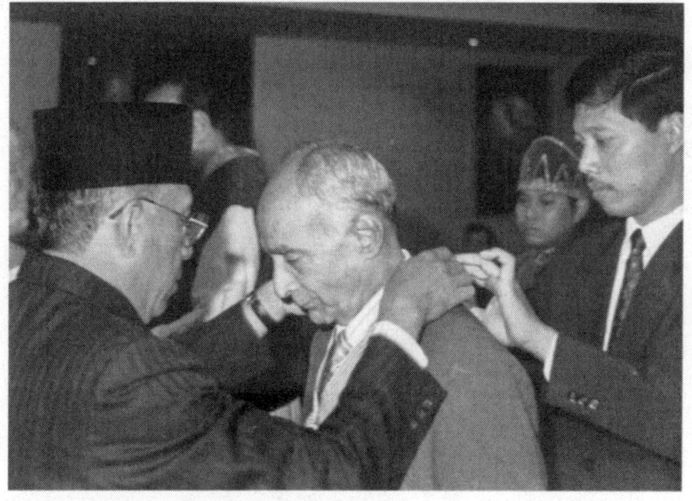

PRS Mani receiving the Order of Merit (shown above) from the Government of Indonesia on December 12, 1995

Following his final retirement in 1977, PRS spent his days in Bangalore with Saraswathi, contributing to seminars and penning articles and books, while, as always, reading historical and philosophical works in a variety of languages (he was fluent in six and spoke several more) and creating a series of increasingly abstract sculptures. He also enjoyed golf and meeting old friends from the worlds he had left behind, but found he had outlived most of them.

On November 1, 1995, Saraswathi passed away. That same year, on December 12, he received the Order of

Merit from the Indonesian government, jointly awarded to him, Nehru (posthumously), Muhammad Yunus, and Biju Patnaik.[3]

Following the loss of his wife, PRS lived on in Bangalore with his sister. The yoga that he had practised almost daily since the age of six kept him fit. He died on August 24, 2011, at the age of 96.

Further Reading

Louis Allen, Burma: *The Longest War, 1941-45*, J.M. Dent and Sons Ltd., 1984.

Peter Ward Fay, *The Forgotten Army: India's Armed Struggle For Independence 1942-1945*, The University of Michigan Press, 1993.

Heather Goodall, *Beyond Borders: Indians, Australians and the Indonesian Revolution, 1939 to 1950*, Amsterdam University Press, 2018.

Diya Gupta, *India in the Second World War: An Emotional History*, Oxford University Press, 2023.

PRS Mani, *The Story of Indonesian Revolution, 1945-1950*, Centre for South and Southeast Asian Studies, University of Madras, 1986.

John Masters, *The Road Past Mandalay: A Personal Narrative*, Harper & Brothers, 1961.

Srinath Raghavan, *India's War: The Making of Modern South Asia, 1939-1945*, Allen Lane, 2016.

William Slim, *Defeat into Victory*, Cassell and Company, 1956.

Kazuo Tamayama and John Nunneley, *Tales by Japanese Soldiers of the Burma Campaign 1942-1945*. Weidenfeld & Nicholson, 2001.

Notes

Introduction

1. Goodall, Heather, and Mark Frost. "The Transnational Mission of an Indian War Correspondent: P. R. S. Mani in Southeast Asia, 1944–1946." *Modern Asian Studies*, (November 2017), pp. 1936–1968, https://doi.org/10.1017/s0026749x16001062.
2. Goodall, Heather. "Conflicted Dispatches: The Writings of P.R.S. Mani, Indian Journalist, Nationalist and British Army Officer in Indonesia, 1945–1949." *Open Publication of UTS Scholars: PRS Mani Collection*, (2014), https://opus.lib.uts.edu.au/handle/10453/28084. Accessed February 18, 2026.
3. Mani, PRS. "Mani: Indian Army Observer (May 20, 1944 – November 1, 1944), Battle of Manipur Stories." *Open Publication of UTS Scholars: PRS Mani Collection*, (July 22, 2014), https://hdl.handle.net/10453/28086. Accessed February 18, 2026; Mani, PRS. "Scripts for Radio Broadcasts Delivered in India about British Army Burma Campaign, 1944." *Open Publication of UTS Scholars: PRS Mani Collection*, (July 22, 2014), https://hdl.handle.net/10453/28087. Accessed February 18, 2026; Mani, PRS. "British Army Dispatches Reporting from Pegu, Burma, prior to Japanese Surrender, 1945." *Open Publication*

of UTS Scholars: PRS Mani Collection, (July 22, 2014), http://hdl.handle.net/10453/28088. Accessed February 18, 2026; Mani, PRS. "British Army Dispatches Reporting from Burma and Singapore, Including Japanese Surrender, 1945." *Open Publication of UTS Scholars: PRS Mani Collection*, (July 22, 2014), https://hdl.handle.net/10453/28089. Accessed February 18, 2026; Mani, PRS. "British Army Dispatches Reporting from Batavia and Surabaya, Indonesia, after Japanese Surrender (Includes Personal Diary Entries), 1945." *Open Publication of UTS Scholars: PRS Mani Collection*, (July 22, 2014), https://hdl.handle.net/10453/28090. Accessed February 18, 2026.

4. Mani, PRS. "Handwritten Diary Entries, 1946." *Open Publication of UTS Scholars: PRS Mani Collection*, (July 22, 2014), https://hdl.handle.net/10453/28092. Accessed February 18, 2026; Mani, PRS. "British Army Dispatches Reporting from Batavia and Surabaya, Indonesia, after Japanese Surrender (Includes Personal Diary Entries), 1945." *Open Publication of UTS Scholars: PRS Mani Collection*, (July 22, 2014), https://hdl.handle.net/10453/28090. Accessed February 18, 2026.
5. Mani, PRS. "India Will Take Care of Her Children Abroad." *Open Publication of UTS Scholars: PRS Mani Collection*, (July 22, 2014), https://hdl.handle.net/10453/28091. Accessed February 18, 2026; Mani, PRS. "Tightening Dutch Grip on Indonesia." *Open Publication of UTS Scholars: PRS Mani Collection*, (July 22, 2014), https://hdl.handle.net/10453/28098. Accessed February 18, 2026.
6. Mani, PRS. "The Story of Indonesian Revolution." *Open Publication of UTS Scholars: PRS Mani Collection*, (July 22, 2014), https://hdl.handle.net/10453/28111. Accessed February 18, 2026.

7. Mani, PRS. *Look Up and Aim High*. Chennai, India, New Century Book House, (2005).
8. "Liddell Hart Centre for Military Archives." *King's College London Archives*, https://archives.kingscollections.org/index.php/liddell-hart-centre-for-military-archives. Accessed February 18, 2026.

Chapter 1: The War from Delhi

1. Mani, PRS. "Mani: Indian Army Observer (20 May 1944 – 1 Nov 1944), Battle of Manipur Stories." *Open Publication of UTS Scholars: PRS Mani Collection*, (July 22, 2014), https://hdl.handle.net/10453/28086. Accessed February 18, 2026; Mani, PRS. "Scripts for Radio Broadcasts Delivered in India about British Army Burma Campaign, 1944." *Open Publication of UTS Scholars: PRS Mani Collection*, (July 22, 2014), http://hdl.handle.net/10453/28087. Accessed February 18, 2026.
2. Personal reminiscence. See also: Zivin, J. "'Bent': A Colonial Subversive and Indian Broadcasting." *Oxford Academic: Past & Present*, (February 1, 1999), pp. 195–220, https://doi.org/10.1093/past/162.1.195.
3. Mani, PRS. *Look Up and Aim High*. Chennai, India, New Century Book House, (2005).
4. Mani, PRS. "Mani: Indian Army Observer (20 May 1944 – 1 Nov 1944), Battle of Manipur Stories." *Open Publication of UTS Scholars: PRS Mani Collection*, (July 22, 2014), https://hdl.handle.net/10453/28086. Accessed February 18, 2026.
5. Allen, Louis. *Burma: The Longest War 1941–1945*. London, UK, Phoenix Press, ([1984] 2000).
6. Personal reminiscence.
7. "'Advice to Surrender/'To You The English Soldiers!', Japanese Propaganda Leaflet, 1944." *Online Collection,*

National Army Museum, https://collection.nam.ac.uk/detail.php?acc=1996-07-76-5. Accessed February 18, 2026.

Chapter 2: Manipur Front

1. Mani, PRS. "Mani: Indian Army Observer (May 20, 1944 – November 1, 1944), Battle of Manipur Stories." *Open Publication of UTS Scholars: PRS Mani Collection*, (July 22, 2014), https://hdl.handle.net/10453/28086. Accessed February 18, 2026; Mani, PRS. "Scripts for Radio Broadcasts Delivered in India about British Army Burma Campaign, 1944." *Open Publication of UTS Radio Broadcasts Delivered in India about British Army Scholars: PRS Mani Collection*, (July 22, 2014), https:// hdl.handle.net/10453/28087. Accessed February 18, 2026.
2. Personal reminiscence.
3. Kellogg, Charles W. "Legions Promenade Down Avenues – into History." *The Roundup*, (March 14, 1946), www.cbi-theater.com/roundup/roundup031446.html. Accessed February 18, 2026.
4. Masters, John. *The Road Past Mandalay: A Personal Narrative.* Bantam Books, (March 1, 1979).
5. Personal reminiscence. Confirmed in: "A SURVEY OF ENEMY OPS TO CAPTURE BASTION ON THE NIGHT 10/11 JUNE." (June 17, 1944). Gracey Collection. Liddell Hart Centre for Military Archives. https://archives.kingscollections.org/index.php/liddell-hart-centre-for-military-archives. King's College London. Accessed February 18, 2026.
6. Personal reminiscence. PRS was together with Steer for months and likely heard it from him. Confirmed in: "REPORT ON OPS BY IFBU". (April 7, 1944). Gracey Collection. Liddell Hart Centre for Military Archives. https://archives.kingscollections.

org/index.php/liddell-hart-centre-for-military-archives. King's College London. Accessed February 18, 2026.

7. The officer in question was a certain Colonel Harvest, as revealed in: "LETTER FROM BRIGADIER STUART GREEVES TO MAJOR-GENERAL DOUGLAS GRACEY". (April 23, 1944.) Liddell Hart Centre for Military Archives. https://archives.kingscollections.org/index.php/liddell-hart-centre-for-military-archives. King's College London. Accessed February 18, 2026.
8. Mani, PRS. "Mani: Indian Army Observer (20 May 1944 – 1 Nov 1944), Battle of Manipur Stories." *Open Publication of UTS Scholars: PRS Mani Collection*, (July 22, 2014), https://hdl.handle.net/10453/28086. Accessed February 18, 2026; Mani, PRS. "Scripts for Radio Broadcasts Delivered in India about British Army Burma Campaign, 1944." *Open Publication of UTS Scholars: PRS Mani Collection*, (July 22, 2014), https://hdl.handle.net/10453/28087. Accessed February 18, 2026.
9. "As Auden showed in his marvelous poem …" was added by the editor.

Chapter 3: Shenam Saddle and Imphal Approaches

1. Mani, PRS. "Mani: Indian Army Observer (20 May 1944–1 Nov 1944), Battle of Manipur Stories." *Open Publication of UTS Scholars: PRS Mani Collection*, (July 22, 2014), https://hdl.handle.net/10453/28086. Accessed February 18, 2026; Mani, PRS. "Scripts for Radio Broadcasts Delivered in India about British Army Burma Campaign, 1944." *Open Publication of UTS Scholars: PRS Mani Collection*, (July 22, 2014), https://hdl.handle.net/10453/28087. Accessed February 18, 2026.
2. PRS only loosely links fanaticism in war with courage, but see: Masters, John. *The Road Past Mandalay: A Personal Narrative.*

Bantam Books, (March 1, 1979), pp. 163 –164.

3. "Gurkhas Advancing with Lee Tanks to Clear the Japanese from Imphal-Kohima Road." *Wikimedia Commons.* https://commons.wikimedia.org/wiki/File:Gurkhas_advancing_with_Lee_tanks_to_clear_the_Japanese_from_Imphal-Kohima_road.jpg. Accessed February 18, 2026 .
4. "Men of the 10th Gurkha Rifles Clearing Enemy Positions on 'Scraggy' Hill, Manipur, 1944." *National Army Museum.* https://collection. nam.ac.uk/detail.php?acc=1998-01-154-5. Accessed February 18, 2026.
5. "Havildar Dhan Singh, Lance-Havildar Dhan Bahadur Gurung and Rifleman Lal Bahadur Rai of the 10th Gurkha Rifles Resting after the Capture of 'Scraggy' Hill, 1944." *National Army Museum.* https://collection.nam.ac.uk/detail.php?acc=1998-01-154-3. Accessed February 18, 2026.
6. "Discarded Japanese Equipment on 'Malta Hill' Seen from 'Scraggy' Hill, Burma, 1944." *National Army Museum,* https://collection. nam.ac.uk/detail.php?acc=1998-01-154-2. Accessed February 18, 2026.

Chapter 4: Ukhrul–Palel Ridge Positions

1. Mani, PRS. "Mani: Indian Army Observer (20 May 1944 – 1 Nov 1944), Battle of Manipur Stories." *Open Publication of UTS Scholars: PRS Mani Collection*, (July 22, 2014), https://hdl.handle.net/10453/28086. Accessed February 18, 2026; Mani, PRS. "Scripts for Radio Broadcasts Delivered in India about British Army Burma Campaign, 1944." *Open Publication of UTS Scholars: PRS Mani Collection*, (July 22, 2014), https://hdl.handle.net/10453/28087. Accessed February 18, 2026.
2. Mani, PRS. "Mani: Indian Army Observer (20 May 1944 – 1 Nov 1944), Battle of Manipur Stories." *Open Publication of*

UTS Scholars: PRS Mani Collection, (July 22, 2014), https://hdl.handle.net/10453/28086. Accessed February 18, 2026; Mani, PRS. "Scripts for Radio Broadcasts Delivered in India about British Army Burma Campaign, 1944." *Open Publication of UTS Scholars: PRS Mani Collection*, (July 22, 2014), https://hdl.handle.net/10453/28087. Accessed February 18, 2026.

Chapter 5: Kyaukse–Meiktila Sector

1. Mani, PRS. "British Army Dispatches Reporting from Pegu, Burma, Prior to Japanese Surrender, 1945." *Open Publication of UTS Scholars: PRS Mani Collection*, (July 22, 2014), https://hdl.handle.net/10453/28088. Accessed February 18, 2026; Mani, PRS. "British Army Dispatches Reporting from Burma and Singapore, Including Japanese Surrender, 1945." *Open Publication of UTS Scholars: PRS Mani Collection*, (July 22, 2014), https://hdl.handle.net/10453/28089. Accessed February 18, 2026.

Chapter 6: Pegu–Rangoon Corridor

1. Mani, PRS. "British Army Dispatches Reporting from Burma and Singapore, Including Japanese Surrender, 1945." *Open Publication of UTS Scholars: PRS Mani Collection*, (July 22, 2014), https://hdl.handle.net/10453/28089. Accessed February 18, 2026.

Chapter 7: Singapore Liberated

1. Mani, PRS. "British Army Dispatches Reporting from Burma and Singapore, Including Japanese Surrender, 1945." *Open Publication of UTS Scholars: PRS Mani Collection*, (July 22, 2014), https://hdl.handle.net/10453/28089. Accessed February 18, 2026.

2. "Signing of the Japanese Surrender at Singapore, 1945." *Wikimedia Commons*, (September 12, 1945), https://commons.wikimedia.org/wiki/File%3ASigning_of_ the_Japanese_Surrender_at_Singapore%2C_1945_ CF720.jpg. Accessed February 18, 2026.
3. Slim, William. *Defeat into Victory: Battling Japan in Burma and India, 1942–1945*. UK, Cooper Square Press, (1956).
4. "Mountbatten Inspects Indian Troops at Singapore 1945." Wikimedia Commons, (1945). https://commons.wikimedia.org/wiki/File:Mountbatten_inspects_Indian_troops_at_Singapore_1945.jpg. Accessed February 18, 2026.
5. "Japanese Soldiers Executing Indian Prisoners of War at Singapore, 1942." Online Collection, National Army Museum, https://collection.nam.ac.uk/detail.php?acc=2009-11-4-25. Accessed February 18, 2026.

Chapter 8: Java Security Operations

1. Mani, PRS. "The Story of Indonesian Revolution." *Open Publication of UTS Scholars: PRS Mani Collection*, (July 22, 2014), https://hdl.handle.net/10453/28111. Accessed February 18, 2026.
2. Mani, PRS. "British Army Dispatches Reporting from Batavia and Surabaya, Indonesia, after Japanese Surrender (Includes Personal Diary Entries), 1945." *Open Publication of UTS Scholars: PRS Mani Collection*, (July 22, 2014), https://hdl.handle.net/10453/28090. Accessed February 18, 2026.

Chapter 9: Surabaya Revolt

1. Mani, PRS. "British Army Dispatches Reporting from Batavia and Surabaya, Indonesia, after Japanese Surrender (Includes Personal Diary Entries), 1945." Open Publication of UTS

Scholars: PRS Mani Collection, (July 22, 2014), https://hdl.handle.net/10453/28090. Accessed February 18, 2026; Mani, PRS. "Handwritten Diary Entries, 1946." Open Publication of UTS Scholars: PRS Mani Collection, (July 22, 2014), https://hdl.handle.net/10453/28092. Accessed February 18, 2026.

2. Kumar, Anu. "As a Fighter and a Peace Broker, an Indian Played a Memorable Role in Indonesia's Freedom Struggle." *Scroll.in*, (October 5, 2024), https://scroll.in/magazine/1073856/as-a-fighter-and-a-peace-broker-an-indian-played-a-memorable-role-in-indonesias-freedom-struggle. Accessed February 18, 2026.
3. Mani, PRS. "India Will Take Care of Her Children Abroad." *Open Publication of UTS Scholars: PRS Mani Collection*, (July 22, 2014), https://hdl.handle.net/10453/28091. Accessed February 18, 2026.
4. Mani, PRS. "British Army Dispatches Reporting from Batavia and Surabaya, Indonesia, after Japanese Surrender (Includes Personal Diary Entries), 1945." *Open Publication of UTS Scholars: PRS Mani Collection*, (July 22, 2014), https://hdl.handle.net/10453/28090. Accessed February 18, 2026; Mani, PRS. "The Story of Indonesian Revolution." *Open Publication of UTS Scholars: PRS Mani Collection*, (July 22, 2014), https://hdl.handle.net/10453/28111. Accessed February 18, 2026; Parrott, J.G.A. "Who Killed Brigadier Mallaby?" *Indonesia*, (October 1975), pp. 87–111, https://doi.org/10.2307/3350997; Goodall, Heather. *Beyond Borders: Indians, Australians and the Indonesian Revolution, 1939 to 1950*. Routledge, (October 1, 2005).
5. "The British Occupation of Java." *Imperial War Museums*, (1945–1989), https://www.iwm.org.uk/collections/item/object/205208436. Accessed February 18, 2026.
6. "Bren Gunners of 3/9th Jat Regiment Cover the Advance of

Their Regiment against Indonesian Nationalists in Surabaya (Soerabaja)." Wikimedia Commons, (November 15–16, 1945), https://commons.wikimedia.org/wiki/File:IWM-SE-5866-Jat-Bren-_gunners-in-Surabaya-194511.jpg. Accessed February 18, 2026.

7. Mani, PRS. "India Will Take Care of Her Children Abroad." *Open Publication of UTS Scholars: PRS Mani Collection*, (July 22, 2014), https://hdl.handle.net/10453/28091. Accessed February 18, 2026.
8. Mani, PRS. "The Story of Indonesian Revolution." *Open Publication of UTS Scholars: PRS Mani Collection*, (July 22, 2014), https://hdl.handle.net/10453/28111. Accessed February 18, 2026.

PRS Mani: A Brief Biography

1. Mani, PRS. *Look Up and Aim High*. Chennai, India, New Century Book House, (2005).
2. Mani, PRS. "Bread and Stone." *Open Publication of UTS Scholars: PRS Mani Collection*, (July 22, 2014), https://hdl.handle.net/10453/28115. Accessed February 18, 2026.
3. Mani, PRS. "Miscellaneous Items Related to Indonesian Government Awards Ceremony in Honour of Jawaharlal Nehru, P.R.S. Mani and Others, 1995." *Open Publication of UTS Scholars: PRS Mani Collection*, (July 22, 2014), https://hdl.handle.net/10453/28116. Accessed February 18, 2026.